ST IGNATIUS
OF LOYOLA

ST IGNATIUS OF LOYOLA

A Pictorial Biography

by

Leonard von Matt
and Hugo Rahner, S.J.

Translated from the German by
John Murray, S.J.

HENRY REGNERY COMPANY
Chicago

This Edition first published in 1956

Henry Regnery Company
20 W. Jackson Blvd.
Chicago 4, Illinois

IMPRIMI POTEST
J. D. Boyle, S.J., Praep. Prov. Angl. Soc. Jesu
Die 21a Martii, 1956

NIHIL OBSTAT
Carolus Davis, S.T.L., *Censor deputatus*
IMPRIMATUR
E. Morrogh Bernard, *Vic. Gen.*
Westmonasterii, die 8a Februarii, 1956

PLATES PRINTED BY IMAGO, ZÜRICH
TEXT PRINTED IN GREAT BRITAIN BY
HAZELL WATSON AND VINEY LTD
AYLESBURY AND LONDON

CONTENTS

ACKNOWLEDGEMENTS

OUR THANKS are due in the first place to His Paternity, the Very Reverend Father John B. Janssens of the Society of Jesus and to his assistants, Father Peter van Gestel and Father Severiano Azcona. For their generous help we thank also the Fathers of the Historical Institute of the Society of Jesus in Rome and of the General Archives of the Order, Fathers Pedro de Leturia, Georg Schurhammer, Josef Teschitel, Ignacio Iparraguirre, E. J. Burrus, all members of the Society.

We should like to express a similar gratitude to Father A. Arana, S.J., at Loyola and to the Directors of Museums, Libraries and Archives, as also to all collaborators in Italy, Spain, France and Switzerland. A special meed of thanks is owed to Father Burkhart Schneider, S.J., in Rome.

Illustrations, presentation and general design: Leonard von Matt, Buchs, Switzerland, by whom all the photographs were taken during the years 1954/55 specially for this book, with the exception of numbers 107–114 which are used by permission of Phil. Giegel, Zürich. The block on the front of the binding shows the first seal of the Society of Jesus.

Text: Rev. Professor Hugo Rahner, S.J., Innsbruck.

Maps: Robert Häsler, Zürich.

This English translation, based on the original German language edition, is issued by arrangement with the original publishers: NZN Buchverlag, Zürich.

This work appears also in French, Italian and Dutch editions, and a separate edition is published in Western Germany.

———

For those readers who are not familiar with the Saint's original writings, it may save some confusion to note that in his diaries Ignatius usually refers to himself in the third person.

THE FAMILY OF LOYOLA

The life and work of St Ignatius Loyola stands deeply embedded in the history of the Church and the culture of the sixteenth century as the structure of his ancestral noble house stands firmly at the heart of the Basque province of Guipúzcoa. His heroic figure needs no legends. And so his life is presented in this volume through the art of photographs which recall the chequered world in which Ignatius lived, and in the text of a biographical study, based for every statement it contains on historical sources, which we possess for Ignatius in abundant measure.

Inigo López de Loyola belongs by both birth and upbringing to one of the four and twenty noble Basque families of Guipúzcoa, which from the earliest times of that people, whose origins are shrouded in mystery, have lived upon their substantial country properties. The first ancestor of the family, of whom there is record in 1180, was Lope de Oñaz, whose castle stood on Oñazmendi, a mountain to the south of Loyola, but has disappeared without trace. The grandson of this Lope married about the year 1260 the heiress Ines de Loyola, and since that time these two family names and their coats-of-arms have remained associated. The grandchildren of this couple are the heroes of the battle of Beotibar (1321) sung of in popular Basque balladry. In addition to other property Beltrán Yánez de Loyola inherited in 1394 the rich patronage of the parish church in nearby Azpeitia, and we know from his will, made in 1405, that at the close of the fourteenth century he had enlarged the family manor he inherited to the dimensions of a fortress with its tower, the walls of which, more than three feet in depth, were able in 1420 to withstand the culverins of his noble enemies. His daughter and heiress, Sancha, married in 1416 Lope García de Lazcano, from ancient Basque stock established as early as 1053 in Inigo de Lazcano. A contemporary said of the two houses: "The house of Loyola is the richest in revenue, actual money, and retinue with the one exception of the house of Lazcano." The son of this marriage was Inigo's grandfather, Juan Pérez de Loyola.

The feuds of the Basque nobility divided into two warring parties, their common struggle against the towns that had been increasing in importance since the fourteenth century, their pride in purity of race, their unassailable Catholic piety and yet their many natural children—this is the wild and haughty background of these remoter ancestors. At the period when Inigo's grandfather was born their social significance was already in decline; they were confronted by the democracy of the cities and the powerful monarchy of Castille. Inigo's own development was profoundly influenced by this change of fortune. Looking back on family history he could write to a nephew in 1539: "Our forbears put all their energy into distinguishing themselves in things which, let us piously hope, were not entirely vain and idle. You must now distinguish yourself in things that have eternal value."

THE FAMILY OF LOYOLA

Notes on the six plates that follow:

1 COAT-OF-ARMS OF THE FAMILY OF LOYOLA

One of the oldest Basque armorial bearings from the beginning of the fourteenth century. In silver a black cauldron, hanging by a chain. To right and left two black wolves rampant.

2 THE MANOR HOUSE OF LOYOLA

The lower portion in masonry from the end of the fourteenth century: the upper in brickwork from 1461. This exterior has remained unchanged. The building has a more or less cubic form, with the sides measuring roughly 50 feet.

3 GOTHIC PORTAL IN MANOR HOUSE

The shield over the door was transferred from the older and simpler building to the new house. The modern marble tablet commemorates the year of Inigo's birth, 1491, and the conversion which he experienced here in 1521.

4 BRIDGE ACROSS THE RIVER UROLA (15TH CENTURY)

This was the point of assembly for the troops of the Lords of Loyola in the event of war In the background is seen the present Jesuit college which contains the old manor house.

5 TYPICAL CONSTRUCTION OF A BASQUE NOBLEMAN'S CASTLE

The house, Moyica, in Vergara. From it we may gather the impression that the house of Loyola, now included within the framework of the Jesuit college, would originally have given.

6 DOORWAY OF THE CHAPEL OF ST JOHN OF OÑAZ

Here stood the house of the Lords of Oñaz. There are no remains.

1 ▷

2 ▷

3

INIGO'S HOME

On July 31st 1456—exactly one hundred years before the death in Rome of the Loyola who became a saint—there hung on the church doors in Azcoitia a declaration of war. It was issued by the reunited parties of the nobility of Guipúzcoa against the eight associated cities of the province. Inigo's grandfather, Juan Pérez, Lord of the battlemented castle of Loyola, had undersigned the declaration: "When the prescribed term is reached, we shall smite and slay you, we shall do you every hurt as enemies of the King, we shall make your blood flow in streams till your souls depart from your bodies, we shall occasion you every damage and every distress in our power."

With good reason a Basque historian could write: "The Loyolas were one of the most disastrous families our country had to endure, one of those Basque families that bore a coat-of-arms over its main doorway, the better to justify the misdeeds that were the tissue and pattern of its life." So began the struggle in the course of which the burghers of Azpeitia and Azcoitia, with the approval of Henry IV, King of Castille, conquered the stronghold that lay between them and threatened them both, and razed the castle down to its second storey. The rebellious Don Juan Pérez was banished by the King in April 1457 for four years, to the distant front against the Moors in Andalusia, "for the defence of the Catholic Faith, that you may wage war there with your followers and weapons and at your own expense against the enemies of the Faith". The energies of the Loyola might work themselves out less dangerously. On his return in 1461 the Lord of Loyola received permission from the King to reconstruct his house, but with less formidable material, with brickwork, which —the first of its kind in Guipúzcoa—betrayed the delicate Mudéjar style and Moorish influence from Castille. The parent house of Loyola still stands, a symphony in Basque masonry, ancient armorial bearings and Spanish elegance. The local rebellion made no alteration in the loyalty of Loyola to the royal house of Castille. Already the grandfather of Juan Pérez and his son, who died in early years, had fought the traditional enemy, the Moors, in Castille and

Andalusia. In 1475 the Lords of Loyola, Don Juan Pérez and his son, Beltrán, swore their oath of fealty to the royal consorts, Ferdinand and Isabella, on the field of Azcoitia. Within the castle were preserved in stout oak chests the royal confirmation of their possessions, wedding settlements and testaments. Young Beltrán was a gallant soldier who served for several years under the king of Castille and Aragon. Loyalty to the Crown was a living tradition in the Loyola household. On one occasion, decades afterwards, Ignatius was proudly able to remind the Emperor, Charles V, of the services rendered by his ancestors.

Beltrán de Loyola was Inigo's father. As a young man he married in nearby Azcoitia Doña Marina Saénz de Licona. The marriage agreements, dated July 13th 1467, are still extant. The father of the bride was the Crown lawyer, held in high esteem at the Castilian court, Dr Martín de Licona, generally known from his birthplace as Doctor Ondarroa. In this busy port stood the Licona family house, and that was where Marina had been born. Her mother was Doña Gracia Saénz de Balda, niece of the last male representative of the line. He too was one of those banished in 1457 and he had died in Seville. Through the Balda branch the house of Loyola became related to the Counts of Onate, from the stock of the Guevara, and to the family of Manrique de Lara, which from 1482 bore the rank of Dukes of Nájera. In October 1459 the wealthy Licona purchased the property and, later, the ecclesiastical privileges of the Balda family in Azcoitia. To his daughter Marina he gave a wedding present of 1,600 gold ducats of Aragonese mintage, and the young bride made her entry into the rebuilt house of Loyola, where her parents-in-law handed her chests piled high with silverware and linen. But the finest gift that Marina brought with her was her deep Catholic faith. She was well known for her unquestioning reverence for the Holy See, and for her zeal in taking part in the solemn services of the patronal churches of Azpeitia and Azcoitia. Her family has the additional merit of having introduced into the Basque country the spirit of the great Cardinal Cisneros through their foundation of the reformed Franciscan friary in Sasiola. It was this that inspired Inigo's cousin, Maria López de Emparán, to establish soon afterwards the convent for Tertiaries in Azpeitia to which Inigo was later able to render great services.

[4]

Marina brought into the world seven sons and four daughters. The last of these, an almost unexpected child, coming after twenty-four years of wedlock, was born on a day unknown in 1491. This was Inigo López, Saint Ignatius. In solemn procession he was carried to Azpeitia to the Tower of Insola, where the Loyolas were in the habit of changing into their church dresses, and from there to the patronal church of St Sebastián de Soreasu. The parish priest, Juan de Zabala, baptised the last-born of the manor family with the name, much loved in the Basque country, of Inigo, after the saintly Benedictine Abbot, Eneco of Oña. It was only forty years later, during his student years at Paris, that Inigo, in addition to his baptismal name, adopted the similar and more familiar name of Ignatius. In his Roman period he called himself simply Ignatius.

While the tiny Inigo lay in his cradle, Royal Spain flung open the doors of a New World. On January 8th 1492, the Spanish royal consorts rode victorious into Granada. On August 3rd of the same year, Columbus's caravel, the *Santa Maria*, took to the sea to discover far distant kingdoms. The storm of the new era blew inland across Guipúzcoa. Inigo's father had battled valiantly in the crusade against the Moors. In 1493 the eldest son, Juan Pérez, equipped a vessel in Zumaya, with 85 fully armed men, to join the escort for the second voyage of Columbus. He died in 1496 a hero's death, in the campaign which won for Spain the kingdom of Naples. Another brother, Hernando by name, went to America in 1510 and fell there on royal service. The family estate descended to the second son, Martín García. On September 11th 1498, in the royal palace of Ocaños he married his bride—a young woman beloved of Queen Isabella, the richly dowered Magdalena de Araoz. Among the wedding presents was the beautiful picture of Our Lady's Annunciation for which Magdalena had a shrine constructed in Loyola. Inigo's mother must have died shortly before this marriage: the sister-in-law he loved all his life became the guardian of Inigo's boyhood years. One of his other brothers, Pero López, by an old family tradition was destined for the ecclesiastical state; the intention was to give him the rich parish benefice of Azpeitia. This brother in clerical garb was indeed no model for Inigo; we shall see the common crimes into which they fell together. The brother died as parish priest of Azpeitia in 1529 and left behind four children. Judged by the manners of the time this was nothing extraordinary. There is written evidence to show that Inigo's father, and his brothers, Juan and Martín, each left two illegitimate children.

It was in this family with its blend of unassailable faith, unswerving loyalty to the Crown, and undisciplined natural vitality that Inigo grew up. "He was brought up pious and noble", an old source declares. But all the same more attention was given at Loyola to purity of race and faith than to the care of morals. With just as much reason could the old chronicle of the Society of Jesus that was to come write as follows: "Inigo's upbringing was what was more or less customary in those days and with those customs: more in the spirit of the world than the spirit of God."

INIGO'S HOME

Notes on the six plates that follow:

7   THE CLIFFS OF THE BASQUE COAST

Sunset on the Bay of Ondarroa. This access to the sea gave the able Basque seamen their opportunities for commerce with other countries and encouraged them to make long voyages overseas.

8   THE HOME TOWN OF HIS MOTHER'S FAMILY

Ondarroa is in the Basque province of Vizcaya. The parish church of Our Lady was begun in 1480, after the marriage of Inigo's parents. The family house of the Liconas stands in the tangled streets of the old town.

9   GOTHIC ENTRANCE GATE OF THE LICONA HOUSE

The Licona family transferred itself here in 1414 from its original home in Lequeitio. Its armorial bearings consist of a blue background and against this an anchor cross in gold, ending in a grapnel. The house, called in its description Torre (Tower) de Licona, shows again the typical form of a house of the Basque nobility.

10   THE SMALL FRANCISCAN CONVENT OF ST FRANCIS OF SASIOLA

Situated between Ondarroa and Deva, and founded in 1503 by Juan Pérez de Licona, Inigo's uncle.

11   HOUSE OF A BASQUE PEASANT

The free Basque peasant is established like a lord among his woods and fields. Centuries back, before the building of the manor house, the original seat of the Loyolas may have been very similar to this.

12   DOORWAY OF THE HOUSE OF THE BALDAS IN AZCOITIA

From 1459 the Licona family lived in this house, and here was celebrated the wedding of Inigo's parents in 1467. In the alcove is the coat-of-arms of the Balda family, but by that time the male line was extinct.

INIGO THE BASQUE

Immediately after his birth his parents handed over the infant Inigo to the charge of a peasant woman living near the castle, who reared him with her own children. Very soon the son of the master was happily running around with the peasant children; among the apple orchards in the valley, on hillsides, or under the shade of the mighty oak-trees near the castle, playing by the hounds' kennels or near the smithies belonging to his father which forged the metal for breastplates, lances and ships' anchors that were well known throughout Spain. Here he learnt to talk in Basque. In the ten hermitages dependent on his father he sang the old folk-songs and from the peasants he heard the pungent proverbs in which so much of the wisdom and experience of his own people was distilled. The neatly built, fair-haired youth belonged heart and soul to his stock, of which a Spanish poet once wrote: "They dwell on the iron mountains, strong in action and silent of word, and with their iron Spain has won her gold." Inigo in his leathern sandals was very adept in performing the country dances. As a grown man he once danced to cheer up a melancholy friend just as on another occasion in his later years as General of the Society he amused himself eating four roast chestnuts because they recalled his much-loved homeland. But for Inigo the happy days of first youth came to their end. A private tutor from one of the seven benefices of the patronal church taught him to read and write in Spanish. To be sure Inigo's Spanish remained always coloured by the ancient, mysterious language of his childhood days. Perhaps his parents had thought of a clerical career for him, for as a boy he received the tonsure, though his name never appeared in the episcopal register of Pamplona. Already his own leanings in Loyola were towards the military glory of his brothers. A hard-headed and laconic Basque—that is what Inigo remained his whole life long. Of his General one of his companions would one day say: "You must realise that Father Ignatius is a kindly and virtuous man. But he is a Basque; when once he has put an idea into his head, well—that's the end of the matter." Oak and iron are the symbols of this people that gave us Ignatius.

INIGO THE BASQUE

Notes on the eight plates that follow:

13   BAPTISTRY OF THE PARISH CHURCH IN AZPEITIA

Over the font in the middle is a statue of St Ignatius with the Basque inscription: "Emenchen batiatuba naiz" (Here was I baptised). When the church was reconstructed in 1569 the late Gothic Baptistry was left untouched. The family tombs of Oñaz and Loyola on either side of the High Altar were, however, removed.

14   VIEW FROM THE CASTLE TOWARDS THE MOUNTAIN IZARRAITZ

The apple orchards in the valley of Urola are famous. The castle was formerly situated in the midst of thick belts of fruit trees.

15   PEASANT HOUSE AT EGUIBAR

Not far from the castle may still be found the cottage of the ironworker, Errazti, whose wife, Maria de Garin, was Inigo's foster-mother.

16   A BASQUE FARMHOUSE

At least twenty farmhouses of this kind belonged to the Loyola estate and gave a yearly yield of some 700 ducats.

17   A SPAN OF OXEN PLOUGHING

Basque peasants hold even today to their traditional methods of agriculture.

18   A YOKE OF OXEN

The brown-black oxen make a colourful picture with their harness of white sheepskin and the scarlet tassels that dangle from the yoke-pad.

19   CHARACTERISTIC BASQUE HARNESS

The Basque peasant can give to the tools and trappings of everyday life a certain style of his own, strongly influenced by tradition. The harness is here seen spread out on the steps of the college at Loyola.

20   ALBARCAS

The footwear of Basque peasants remains what it was in Inigo's time: sandals of oxen leather tied with laces over stockings of homespun wool.

13 ▷

THE YOUNG SQUIRE OF ARÉVALO

Probably in 1506, certainly before his father's death in the beginning of 1507, a tempting item of news reached Loyola. Juan Velázquez de Cuéllar, master of the royal treasury, a man known all over Spain and a close friend of Inigo's father, asked Beltrán de Loyola to send him one of his sons that he might bring him up as his own child in his splendid household and later on introduce him to the great world of the Court. Inigo set off with genuine delight, riding through Burgos and Valladolid to Arévalo where Velázquez resided. Ten decisive years were spent by the young nobleman as page and elegant young courtier in near attendance upon his master, who also exercised authority in Madrigal and Olmedo and frequently accompanied the monarch on his journeys to the Cortes or to Tordesillas to visit Juana, his mad daughter. The Treasurer's wife, Maria de Velasco, and her religious mother, Maria de Guevara, were related to Inigo's own mother, and their influence brought the youthful Loyola into contact with that noble spirit which the late Queen and the great Cardinal Cisneros had cultivated at the Court.

However, there were other things in the court atmosphere for a growing nobleman to learn. Like every healthy youngster Inigo played his pranks and his Guevara aunt is supposed once to have told him: "Inigo, you'll never learn sense until someone gives you a good drubbing." His carefree playmate in those days, Alonso de Montalvo, affirmed afterwards that Inigo's only desire in those days was for a military career; and Ribadeneira, his first biographer, declares that he was "a gay and elegant fellow" and "a friend of smart clothes and good living". He prided himself on his fashionably brushed blond hair and the neatness both of his dress and his fingernails. Maria de Velasco then had the task of inventing games and entertainments for King Ferdinand's second wife, Germaine de Foix, and Inigo had frequently waited as a page at table during the queen's boisterous banquets. Inigo discovered his life's ideal in those intricate and passionate romances, in which the deeds of valour and the love adventures of Amadis and Tristan were so vividly pictured, that, as he confessed subsequently, his imagination was entirely filled with them. But in Arévalo Inigo not only acquired that delicate feeling for courtly culture, which broke through again in the serene days of his later years. Here also began his experience of sin.

THE SQUIRE OF ARÉVALO

Notes on the eight plates that follow:

21 CITY GATE OF MADRIGAL DE LAS ALTAS TORRES (MADRIGAL OF THE HIGH TOWERS)

Queen Isabella, known in Spain as Isabel la Católica, was born in this city. The master of the royal treasury, Don Juan Velázquez, resided occasionally in the palace. The church of St Nicholas that is glimpsed through the doorway is one of the best examples of the early Mudéjar style.

22–23 CITY OF MADRIGAL ON THE CASTILIAN PLATEAU

What a contrast is this high plateau, splendid in isolation, with the fertile hill country of the Basques!

24 ARÉVALO, THE CHIEF RESIDENCE OF THE GRAND TREASURER

To the left, the Fortress Tower of St Martin. In the centre, the church of St Michael, constructed on the foundations of a mosque. This little city played an important rôle in the history of the royal house of Castille.

25 LA LUGAREJA NEAR ARÉVALO

A church of a religious order, begun in the 13th century and not completed. The Moorish-Roman brickwork (in Mudéjar or Morisko style) set amid the simple cottages recalls the heroic age of the Christian reconquest of Spain.

26–27 PICTURE OF A GRAND TOURNAMENT

Taken from a history of the Emperors dedicated to Charles V. The work, printed at Augsburg in 1527, is in the library of the Escorial.

28 THE POPULAR ROMANCES OF CHIVALRY

Amadis of Gaul, the first Spanish edition of which appeared in 1508, was one of Inigo's favourite books. The copy shown in the photograph dates from 1531 and is practically identical with the original edition. As one further example of these numerous romances the photograph shows a 1528 edition of the work, "The gallant knight, Don Tristan de Leonis, and his deeds of derring-do".

[10]

Turnier

Amadis de gaula .:.

Os q̃tro libros de Amadis de gaula nueuamẽte impssos z hystoriados ẽ Seuilla.

Libro del esforça=do cauallero dõ tristan de leonis y de sus grãdeshechos en armas.

THE WILD SOLDIER

That is how one man who knew him spoke of Inigo at this period. The young squire had developed into an officer full of life and enjoying every moment of it. When he read accounts of his brothers' prowess in arms, this was how he reacted, as he confessed later: "He took pleasure in the exercise of weapons and nourished a strong but vain personal desire to win military renown." His faith remained unshaken, however, and before fighting a duel he might throw off a pious poem to Our Lady or to the patron of the Fortress church of Arévalo, St Peter of the Sword. At the same time, as those who were afterwards his close friends said tactfully but with complete truth, he was "reckless at games, in adventures with women, in brawls and deeds of arms. He was assailed and overcome by temptations of the flesh."

It is not astonishing, therefore, that the figure of the future saint should be brought home vividly for the first time out of the documents of an obscure legal process, in which he became involved along with his clerical brother during a visit to his Basque home at carnival time, 1515. The documents, although incomplete, make it clear that it was a case of "nightly excesses, serious and grave misdemeanours" which the brothers had "systematically and cunningly carried through". A description is added of the offending officer: "He is in the habit of going round in cuirass and coat of mail, wears his hair long to the shoulder, and walks about in a two-coloured, slashed doublet with a bright cap: no one has ever seen him in clerical attire". Nevertheless, Inigo claimed the privileges of the tonsure to put himself beyond the reach of the civil court. It is reasonably evident that the painful affair was hushed up at the episcopal court in Pamplona because of the influence of his master, the Treasurer.

In these years of "his youth's misguided steps", as Inigo termed them in his later shame, he cultivated a romantic affection for a high-born lady, just as his hero, Amadis, had done for the Lady Oriana. This little secret of the heart was half revealed in his own words: "The lady was no ordinary noblewoman, no

[11]

countess and no duchess, her position was even more exalted." She was in fact
—so competent authorities have suggested—the Infanta Catherine, youngest
sister of the Emperor Charles. She had passed her gloomy youth at Tordesillas
in the palace where her mad mother was imprisoned. Inigo had frequently seen
her from a distance, for his master's wife, Maria de Velasco, was very popular
there and had shown herself a true friend to the princess. Subsequently Inigo
did penance unto tears for his years at Arévalo.

THE WILD SOLDIER

Notes on the six plates that follow:

29   ARMOUR OF A SPANISH OFFICER
From the Royal Armoury at Madrid: beginning of the sixteenth century.

30–31 THE CASTLE OF ARÉVALO
Situated on a hill at the Northern outskirts of the city, the castle was connected by a sub-
terranean passage with the Fortress church of St Peter: this church has now disappeared.

32   THE LADY OF HIS HEART
The Infanta Catherine, painted by the Portuguese artist, Carvalho, as St Catherine. The picture
is in the Prado, at Madrid.

33   ACCOUTREMENT OF A DISTINGUISHED OFFICER
Two specially fine pieces of armour from the Royal Armoury at Madrid. Beginning of the
sixteenth century. With their exquisite workmanship they fit admirably into that dream world
of courtly romances that so fascinated Inigo.

34   MOORISH DECORATION FROM TORDESILLAS
The roof of the side chapel in the church of the Poor Clares at Tordesillas. Near it once stood the
palace in which Queen Juana was incarcerated. This magnificent work, from the beginning of
the sixteenth century, combines a Moorish style with the pictures of Christian saints. It represents in its full richness that Mudéjar manner which in a more modest way had influenced the
reconstruction of the castle of Loyola.

29 ▷

30 ▷
31

ALLEGIANCE TO THE KING

The happy days at Arévalo came to a sudden end. Inigo learnt for the first time how fleeting can be courtly favour. After the death of King Ferdinand, his grandson, Charles, handed over the cities that Velázquez held in fief, as a widow's pension to Germaine de Foix. The Royal Treasurer rightly judged this to be a breach of the liberties secured by charter and he set the castle of Arévalo in a state of defence against the Regent, Cardinal Cisneros. Till March 1517 the struggle continued for the possession of the city, carried on with legal arguments and with crossed swords. Inigo fought gallantly in its defence. When the aged Velázquez, now weary and reduced to povery, yielded, Inigo's career at court was finished. Velázquez died in August 1517 at Madrid. Maria de Velasco gave Inigo a present of 500 gold pieces and two horses. Now he had to look for another master. Three years subsequently, however, King Charles fully justified the defence of Arévalo. Inigo's first campaign was therefore a loyal rebellion for his King.

The son of Loyola soon found this new master in the person of his relative, Antonio de Manrique, Duke of Nájera and since 1516 Viceroy of Navarre, a mighty liege lord who from his own estates could put 3,000 men and 700 horsemen into the field in the service of the crown. At about the same time, in September 1517 the young Charles came from Flanders to Spain to claim his inheritance. In February 1518 the Cortes assembled in Valladolid, at its head the seven grandees of Castille with their splendid retinues. In the suite of the Duke of Nájera there would have ridden, without any doubt, Don Inigo. The high nobility swore their oath of fealty to the monarch. Inigo's brother, Martín García, was there and on March 5th 1518, in the name of the King and Juana, his mother, he received permission to entail his Basque estate. During the night from the 12th to the 13th of March, King Charles had his young sister, Catherine, removed from the gloomy castle of Tordesillas without the knowledge of the mad mother. The following day a grand tournament was staged in the square in front of the Royal Palace in Valladolid, which the little lady of Inigo's heart could admire from the palace balcony. It was indeed a great day for her devotee, inflamed with the fantastic tales of Amadis. On either side rode five and twenty knights confronting one another, Spaniards and Flemings, and each strove stubbornly to "distinguish himself in the royal service". Charles himself was one of the combatants.

Behind the brilliant façade of this day were looming dark questionings. The Spaniards, proud of their own land, mistrusted the Flemish strangers, whom the young King allowed too large an influence in his government. Shortly after the King's departure flared up the revolt of the so-called Comuneros. But the Duke of Nájera was among the unswerving supporters of the King. With him was Inigo of Loyola.

ALLEGIANCE TO THE KING

Notes on the four plates that follow:

35–36 A KING'S ARMOUR

It was in this magnificence that Inigo first saw his young monarch, later the Emperor Charles V, as he entered Valladolid in 1518. This splendid masterpiece of German metal work is today the central exhibit in the Madrid armoury.

37 COURTYARD OF ST GREGORY'S COLLEGE IN VALLADOLID

This Dominican college with its famous interior courtyard stands near the square in front of the Royal Palace, which itself has been completely reconstructed. It was here that the Spanish nobles assembled before their acts of homage and the grand tournaments.

38 THE MAGNIFICENT FAÇADE OF ST GREGORY'S COLLEGE IN VALLADOLID

The very exaggeration in this masterpiece of late Spanish Gothic expresses the immense self-confidence of the land that had become so rich. The dream world of the romances of chivalry is here turned to stone. In the centre stands forth the coat-of-arms of united Spain. Inigo's forbears had fought for this reunion.

35 ▷

FACING GREAT RESPONSIBILITIES

All too soon must this allegiance demand the sacrifice of blood. In the service of the Viceroy Inigo was fashioned into mature manhood. The kingdom of Navarre, that offered an open door to French invasion, was conquered by Spain and in 1515 solemnly incorporated in the reunited kingdom. Martín García de Loyola had fought gallantly in the campaign. It was the responsibility of the Viceroy to construct a fortress in Pamplona, where the feeble fortifications had not been fully reinforced by 1521. The party of the King of Navarre and, behind it, the French King, Francis, had only one objective in these years: the reconquest of the lost kingdom for its hereditary ruler, Henri d'Albret. In Pamplona the Spaniards were detested and had to be on their guard. Years afterwards, a son of the Duke of Nájera could recall: "I saw Inigo with my own eyes in Pamplona, as a mob of men came through a narrow street, attacked him and pressed him against a wall. But he drew his dagger and chased them down the street. If he hadn't been held back, he would have killed some of them or been himself killed."

Meanwhile out of the movement of the Comuneros had developed a kind of social revolution. Even in small Nájera the ordinary folk rose against the hereditary lordship of the Duke. Such a situation so near to the frontiers of the Basque lands, as the Viceroy wrote to the Emperor, was dangerous in the extreme. The Duke felt himself compelled to take the most severe measures. In September 1520 Nájera was stormed by his troops and, in accordance with the rules of the age, was sacked. Inigo was present. But "though he might have taken a considerable share of the booty, it seemed to his great and noble heart an unworthy thing to do, and he took nothing at all". That is the report of one of his close friends. It was the same Inigo, of whom it was stated, even in his sinful years, that he had never lied nor blasphemed.

Something now occurred which lets one recognize the Ignatius of the future. There was ferment even in the province of Guipúzcoa which till then had remained loyal to the crown. The whole of the Northern front facing France was endangered. Commissioned by the Viceroy, the Basque Inigo succeeded in calming his people. That showed, in the words of one of his own friends, that he was already what he would be later: "ingenious and skilful in affairs of this world, and very clever in the handling of men, particularly when there was question of smoothing out strife and discord."

This special responsibility in the Basque country was only a short interlude; soon weapons would speak in Pamplona.

FACING GREAT RESPONSIBILITIES

Notes on the six plates that follow:

39   NAVARRETE, THE SEAT OF THE DUKES OF NÁJERA

Situated on the borders of the Basque country and Old Castille, in the famous wine district of Rioja. The hill overlooking the town was crowned by the castle, now destroyed, in which the family of Manrique had lived since 1380. Subsequently, Inigo was responsible for the repair of a picture of Our Lady in the church.

40   THE CITY OF NÁJERA

From 1482 onwards the family of Manrique took its ducal title from the city. Their castle no longer exists. The massive church of Santa Maria la Real, built in the fifteenth century, belonged to a monastery founded by King García IV of Navarre in 1052.

41   THE DOORWAY OF THE KINGS, THE ROYAL PORTAL

Over this splendid late Gothic doorway to the cloister there stand out, now peacefully united, the two coats-of-arms of Navarre-Evreux and Castille-León. At the time that Inigo saw these armorial shields, war between the two crowns had burst into flames—the war that was to be decisive in his own life.

42   STATUE OF A KNIGHT FROM THE ROMANCE WORLD OF AMADIS

This imaginative statue of King García IV has stood since 1492 behind the abbot's throne in the church choir.

43   THE BURIAL CRYPT OF THE DUKES OF NÁJERA

Don Pedro Manrique, known as the Brave, who died in 1515, established this burial crypt. He was the father of the Don Antonio whom Inigo served. He was regarded throughout Castille as a model of knightly virtue.

44   THE MONASTERY CLOISTER

Built in the years in which Inigo lived in Nájera, its blend of late Gothic and Renaissance elements makes it one of the finest examples of the "plateresque" style. The blend of styles reflects the changing age.

[16]

WHIT MONDAY, 1521

Meanwhile the whole of Spain had been set on fire by the torch of the Comuneros rebellion. Pamplona was emptied of troops. True, the battle of the bridge at Durana, in April 1521, in which Inigo took part, had secured the Basque provinces against the revolutionaries. But now France thought the moment had come herself to strike: Navarre must be taken back from the King of Spain whom shortly before the German electors had chosen as Emperor. In May 1521 an army of 12,000 men under the leadership of the Lord of Esparros, André de Foix, gathered together to attack Pamplona. In the city there were only a thousand weary militiamen, with nineteen pieces of artillery in the citadel. In deep bewilderment the Duke of Nájera hastened to Burgos to summon assistance, leaving the command to Frances de Beaumont in the city itself, and in the citadel to the Mayor, Herrera. A messenger rode post haste to Guipúzcoa where Inigo was at the time, and appealed to the loyal province for immediate help.

Martín García and his brother Inigo hurried with their soldiers at double speed to Pamplona, and on May 19th they were in front of the city walls. However, the fickle burghers of the town had made up their minds to surrender. After lengthy negotiations at the town gate, Martín García rode away with his followers, thoroughly disillusioned. Inigo reacted differently. At full speed he galloped into the city with a handful of companions. There followed more negotiations, this time with Beaumont, himself inclined to agree to the surrender. Blazing with indignation at so much cowardice, Inigo established himself firmly in the citadel.

That same evening the advance guard of the French entered the city, the main body joining them on the day following. Herrera's opinion was that any resistance in the citadel was madness. In the war council and in negotiations with the French Inigo was spokesman. He had only one theme: defence or death, and honour before all else. Herrera gave in to him; the French attack commenced.

Inigo had no illusions about the seriousness of the hour. Since no priest was available he made confession of his many sins to one of his comrades-in-arms in the Lady chapel. The French cannon began to thunder; the bombardment went on for full six hours. Then came the stroke which Inigo was never to forget: "A cannon shot hit his leg and broke it, and because the shot reached the inner side of the one leg it damaged the other as well." Once he had fallen, the citadel garrison surrendered to the French. It was Whit Monday, May 20th 1521.

WHIT MONDAY, 1521

Notes on the eight plates that follow:

45   THE OLD CITY WALLS OF THE FORTRESS OF PAMPLONA

Above the walls rises the Barbazana chapel, built by Bishop Arnauld de Barbazan after 1317. It belongs to the beautiful cloister that is attached to the Cathedral.

46   THE CAPITANIA GENERAL, RESIDENCE OF THE VICEROY

During his period of service under the Duke of Nájera Inigo was mostly stationed here.

47   OLD STONE BRIDGE IN FRONT OF THE CITY

The victorious troops rode into the city over this bridge which crosses the River Arga.

48   CHOIR SCREEN IN THE CATHEDRAL

This choir screen, a masterpiece of skilled iron work, was completed by the French craftsman, Guillaume Ervenat, in 1517.

49   THE OLD CRUCIFIX "CHRISTO ANTIGUO"

A late Gothic wood carving of the fifteenth century. Behind the crucifix are the pictures of the prophets. The feet of Christ are encased in silver and are kissed by the faithful in pious devotion.

50–51   ROYAL TOMBS IN THE CATHEDRAL

The alabaster sarcophagus of King Charles III of Navarre and his spouse, Leonora of Castille. The work was finished in 1426. In 1425, on the death of this sovereign who had begun the construction of the cathedral in 1397, Navarre was torn asunder through party strife and was fought for both by France and Castille. This situation is symbolised in the dogs fighting for a bone and the monks that stand mourning round the monument.

52   DOORWAY BETWEEN CATHEDRAL AND CLOISTER

The statue of Our Lady in the finest French Gothic is, like the cloister itself, older than the cathedral. In this cloister the Duke of Nájera received the oaths of fealty of the different social orders.

45 ▷

HOME TO LOYOLA

While the French in the excitement of victory rushed madly Southwest towards
Logroño and Castille, the garrison that remained behind in Pamplona treated
their foe with knightly courtesy. There is evidence that gallant Loyola was
brought to the special notice of the Lord of Esparros. He was searched for in
the citadel and carefully brought to safety. This precaution was necessary
since the resentful victors had killed several of the vanquished as the defeated
garrison withdrew. Years afterwards Inigo recalled with what "courtesy and
kindliness" he had been treated. Generously he presented his sword and
sword-belt to the Frenchmen who tended him. Doctors did their best to set
the broken limb and took care of him for two weeks. Then a litter was prepared to transport the wounded man over the mountains to his homeland in
Loyola. There he would have the best chance of recovery.

For a full fortnight the agonizing journey continued. Over the heights of
Lizarraga the way descended to Ozaeta where the sick man, racked with fever,
had the respite of a few days of rest. Then over the well-loved hills to Guipúzcoa.
They no doubt chose this roundabout way to avoid the streets and villages
occupied by the French troops. In Anzuola they halted at the house of Inigo's
sister. Soon the sorry procession reached the bridge of Loyola and the Gothic
doorway of the castle. In the meantime Martín García had sallied out with his
troops for one last desperate stand against the French, and it was his sister-in-
law, Magdalena, who with her two grown-up daughters welcomed Inigo at his
home-coming. She prepared for him the finest room in the upper storey of the
castle.

What were Inigo's thoughts throughout this painful journey? Maybe before
he left Pamplona he had learnt what certain gentlemen of the government in
Burgos thought about the fall of the citadel. They spoke of it as "the greatest
treason in the world" and threatened to write to the Emperor advising him to
behead the commandant. But even this would not have shaken him in his
resolve again to distinguish himself in the service of his monarch. From the

first moment he was back in Loyola the one thing which gave him courage was his determination to recover full health. Doctors and surgeons were summoned from many centres. The case was desperate. It may have been the clumsiness of the doctors in Pamplona or the rough journey home, in any case the bones of his right leg had grown crookedly. "In that case the bone simply would not heal", was the verdict. Inigo drew the only consequence: well, it must be broken again and set afresh. He endured again the torture he had experienced in Pamplona. Later he added his own commentary: "A second time therefore he was forced to put up with this butchery. As with the other pains he had suffered and must later suffer, no word came from his lips; only his clenched fists betrayed his agony."

It all seemed of no avail. As the bell in the hermitage of St John in Oñaz pealed in the feast of the Baptist on June 24th, Inigo's condition made them abandon hope. Death stood before the door of the castle of Loyola.

HOME TO LOYOLA

Notes on the six plates that follow:

53 A VIEW OF THE VALLEY WEST OF PAMPLONA

54–55 A CREST OF HILLS BETWEEN PAMPLONA AND THE BASQUE COUNTRY

The severely injured Inigo was carried by narrow footpaths through the Ollo valley and over the mountains to his home.

56 THE VILLAGE OF GONI

Here began the winding road up to the heights of Lizarraga.

57 THE CITY OF ANZUOLA IN GUIPÚZCOA

Inigo's sister, Magdalena de Gallait-zegui, lived in the manor house of Echandia. On a later visit St Francis Borgia kissed the walls of this house in which Inigo halted on his journey.

58 AN OAK-TREE, THE TYPICAL TREE OF THE BASQUE HOMELAND

Proudly, like the familiar oak of Loyola, these splendid trees stand everywhere in the Basque land.

[20]

58

THE BODY RECOVERS

On the same feast of St John, Inigo received the last Sacraments like a good Christian. The next days were a long struggle with death. On the eve of Saints Peter and Paul the doctor gave him up for lost, unless there were some change before midnight. Later Ignatius was to give an account of this remarkable event: "The sick man had a special devotion to St Peter, and so it pleased Our Lord that precisely at that very midnight his condition started to improve."

Inigo wanted at all costs to recover his full health. He was still wholly determined, as he himself declared, to continue his career in the world. At that moment the bells in Azpeitia were ringing in a victory peal; Martín García, to whom the king had granted the right of primogeniture, came back from the war and described in detail to the excited Inigo how on the day after St Peter's Feast the French had been defeated near Noain, and how since July 5th the Spanish flag waved again over the citadel of Pamplona. A visit paid by his former comrade from Arévalo, Alonso de Montalvo, could only strengthen him in his desire to return as soon as possible to a soldier's life with his old elegance and courage. Alonso could tell him some encouraging stories about Arévalo which throughout had remained loyal to the King, and that the Infanta Catherine and her mother intended to reside there. Inigo was in contact with his master, the Duke of Nájera, who had been brusquely deprived of his post as Viceroy of Navarre; he sent him news of his slow convalescence. For Inigo the doors of his old world remained always open.

There was one obstacle. As the bones of his right leg had knit again it was evident that beneath the knee one piece of bone had pushed itself forward over the other and projected uglily. In consequence the leg was shortened. Inigo was furious. All his hopes of military renown, his dreams as a squire of dames were in the balance. How could he ever again wear a shin-guard for a tournament or the smart riding-boots he took such a pride in, and that had to fit perfectly? There was nothing else for it. The lump of bone must be sawn away. Despite the alarm of his brother and the surgeons Inigo insisted on the operation. He was determined in his own words, "to let himself be martyred; the idea was firmly fixed in his head". He endured the horrible process in silence. With various ointments and a primitive rack they attempted to straighten the leg. For weeks he lay in his corner room in fearful pain and looked up at the oak beams of the roof. "At long last Our Lord restored his health; and the process was so thorough that he felt fully restored to vigour; one difficulty remained, he could not put his weight on his leg. He was forced therefore to remain in bed." These words of his reveal a man's joy in recovery. Before him again stretched the world, with its attraction and appeal.

THE BODY RECOVERS

Notes on the four plates that follow:

59　THE CASTLE THAT WAS HOME

It is now included in the buildings of the Jesuit College and the Basilica. Inigo's sick-room was on the top storey and its windows looked Eastwards towards Azpeitia and Northwards to Mt Izarraitz. The picture shows the East side of the building in sunlight and the North side in shadow.

60　"HERE IGNATIUS GAVE HIMSELF TO GOD"

Inigo's sick-room, converted into a chapel; the roof of heavy oak beams remains unchanged.

61　INIGO'S SICK BELL

There is a pious tradition that Inigo used this bell during his illness.

62　THE REAR VIEW OF THE CASTLE

In the background the Baroque basilica.

[22]

59

THE SOUL IS TRANSFORMED

Autumn came slowly to the Basque land. The patient began to fret at the slowly passing days. There awoke in him the old passion he had felt in Arévalo for those quaint histories of romantic knights. But there was no fashionable reading of that kind to be found in the castle. What his pious sister-in-law found in her cupboards were four leather-bound volumes in which, long ago, a German Carthusian had narrated the life of Christ and, in addition, a thick book of stories of the saints. What a man will read when his leg is in splints! First with reluctance, then with astonishment, and in the end with sheer fascination, Inigo turned the pages. Silently in these hours grace drew near to his sick-bed. A new world opened before his eyes. He read of the true kingdom of God that is greater than any conquest of Granada. He learnt something of the saints' passion for the service of God under the standard of the Cross, of the desert of Onofrius, of the Poverello in Assisi, and of the nightly scourgings of Dominic. That was, in God's name, different from neatly-turned verses to a lady love; that was something more magnificent than any feat of arms for the Emperor. True to his Basque temperament he began to ponder for hours on end. In his mind God and the world were linked together in a remarkable conflict. "What if I were to do the things that Francis and Dominic did?" Then he was again seized by his desire for military honour and his lady's favour. In this hesitation of spirit Inigo made a discovery that was to be decisive in his life. He described it later with a fine sensitiveness. "When he concerned himself with worldly thoughts he found great pleasure in them. But as soon as he tired of the thoughts he grew exhausted and depressed. If, however, he conceived the idea of going to Jerusalem barefoot and feeding on nothing but wild herbs and taking on himself the other penances of which he had read in the saints' lives, then he not only found great comfort as long as he dwelt on such thoughts, but he remained happy and serene even after the thoughts had departed. Gradually he began to recognise the distinction between different spirits, the spirit of the devil and the spirit of God. That was the first reflection he made upon the ways of God." Now, of a sudden, his past appeared shallow and empty. In this new illumination his life of sin stood out in its stark immensity. With unyielding vigour he formed the one paramount resolution: to do penance unto blood, to go as a pilgrim to Jerusalem, as he had learnt from the Carthusian Ludolph, and then to bury himself in some far-away desert. His ideas were still wildly confused and haunted by fancies. But beneath them there already lay the firm and final decision of his life that was to make Inigo a saint of God. "Transformation of soul"—this was how Ignatius himself spoke of these weeks in Loyola.

THE SOUL IS TRANSFORMED

Notes on the six plates that follow:

63   THE LIFE OF CHRIST BY LUDOLPH OF SAXONY (DIED 1377)

Spanish translation in four volumes, 1502 and 1503, which was published in Alcalá with the authority of Cardinal Cisneros. The photograph shows the fourth volume, closed and opened, with the table of contents. Photograph 64 at the top gives the title page of the second volume with a woodcut. The translator, Fray Ambrosio Montesino, O.F.M., dedicated his work to Their Catholic Majesties. Below is the coat-of-arms of united Spain, and the inscription "Vita Christi cartuxano romançido por Fray Ambrosio". Inigo certainly used this edition!

64–65   "FLOS SANCTORUM", LIVES OF THE SAINTS

Composed by James de Voragine, Archbishop of Genoa, who died in 1298. Translated by an unknown hand into Spanish and available in several editions. It is uncertain which of these Inigo would have used. In the photographs is seen the edition of 1524 (The Story of Christ's Passion and the Life of St Dominic), the text of which is in agreement with those of earlier issues.

66   ALTAR OF THE CASTLE CHAPEL AT LOYOLA

In the centre the Flemish picture of the Annunciation that had belonged to Queen Isabella. Originally, as the shield and device proclaim, it had belonged to the Guevara family. To right and left, Saints Catherine of Sienna and Catherine of Alexandria. Above, a late Gothic Pietà.

67   THE HERMITAGE OF OUR LADY AT ELOSIAGA

The church rights of Loyola extended to ten of these hermitages. Here the convalescent Inigo often sought solitude.

68   THE "DEVIL'S SPLIT" IN THE CASTLE WALLS

There exists a legend that at the time of the conversion of Inigo the devil shook the castle to its foundations. The split that runs down the wall is due presumably to one of the not infrequent earthquakes experienced in Guipúzcoa.

63 ▷

64 ▷

65

¶ En esta quarta parte que es cõtinuaciõ dela segũda ꞇ postrimera parte del vita xp̃i Carthuxano romãçado por fray Ambrosio mõtesyno dela ordẽ delos menores: se cõtienẽ los tratados q̃ se sigũe.

¶ Los mysterios dela cena del señor.
¶ Toda su sanctissima passion.
¶ Su gloriosa resurreccion.
¶ Su admirable ascension.
¶ La venida del spiritu sancto sobre los discipulos.
¶ E el estado dela yglesia primitiua.
¶ La assuncion dela virgen maria.
¶ La venida del antecristo ꞇ los fenecimientos del siglo.
¶ La resurreccion general delos muertos.
¶ La venida de xp̃o al juyzio.
¶ El final estado õ todas las criaturas
¶ E otras materias muy excellentes dela fe.

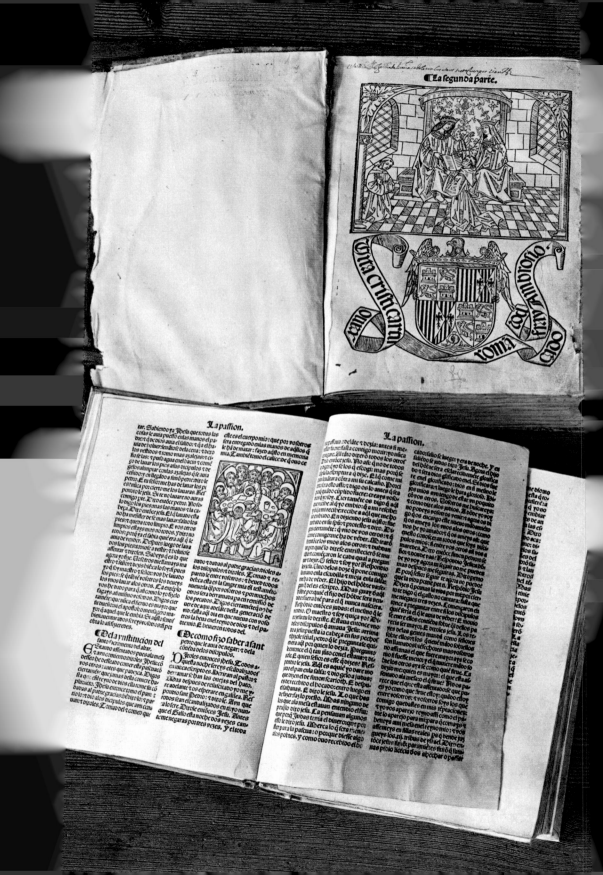

el su braço diestro: z fizieron ay vna yglesia
cathedral muy noble a hō:ra del z viniendo
a roma qriēdo lleuar su cuerpo ala yglia de
sant pedro estuuierō qpos los q lo leuauā z
no pudierō mas yr. y el diablo q estaua ēla
dō:zella comēço a dar bozes: z dezia. En va
no trabajays q no escogio su morada aqui:
mas cerca de su hī:o llorēte z porēde leuarō
el cuerpo alla. Etocādolo la dō:zella luego
fue sana: z sant llo:ēte gozādo se porq venia
a su hī:o: riēdose diole lugar ala otra pte de
derole la mitad ōl sepulcro vazio. y los grie
su sepulcro: z los sus huesos faziēdose a pte
gos qriēdo tomar a sant llorēte cayāse en tie
rra como muertos: mas rogādo el papa: z
la clerezia z todo el pueblo po: ellos: mala
ves tornarō en su memo:ia fasta las bispas
z todos murierō acabo de .x. dias: z los lati
nos q gelo otorgarō fuerō todos flematicos
z avn los cuerpos de ābos los sctōs envno
fuerō los cuerpos glosos de sant llo
enterrados: y entōce oyā vna boz ōl cielo: q
dezia. O roma biē auēturada q encierrā en
vn sepulcro los cuerpos glosos de sant llo
rēte de espana: z de sant esteuā de jheruln. y
cuēta sant augustin q al nōbre de sant esteuā
fuerō seys muertos resucitados. El vno q co
mo estuuiesse muerto asi q ya le atauan los
pulgares: llamādo a sant esteuā luego resu
cito. y otra vezyn nino q lo qbrāto vn carro
po: medio: leuādolo su madre ala yglesia de
sant esteuā murico ay viēdolo todos z ma
rauillando se mucho leuātose sano. Otrosi
quando su madre la su saya ala yglesia desant
enla cibda de oponia murio vna moça: z lle
esteuā: z despues tornādose puso la sobre el
cuerpo ō su fija: y ella luego se leuāto. Otro
sī vn mācebo enessa misma cibdad como su
cuerpomuerto fuesse vntado conel olio ō su
fi
sant esteuā luego resucito. Itē vn nino mu
riēdo leuarō lo alas reliqas de sant esteuā
z llamādo el su nōbre luego fue sano.

La vida de santo Do
mingo: z de sus milagros.

Sancto Domingo fue caudillo:
z padre noble: es llamado dela
o:dē delos p:edicado:es. E fue

de espana: de vna villa que llaman Calero
ga del obispado de osma. E a su padre dire
ron don Felices: z a su madre dona Juana
y ante q el naciese: sono su madre q trayā vn
perrillo enel viētre: z q tenia enla boca vna
hacha ardiēte: el qual salido del viētre entē
dia todo el mūdo: z parescia a vna muger q
fue muy noble: su madrina de domingo. El
nino q auia vna estrella enla frēte que alum
braua todo el mūdo. y el seyēdo nino falla
ron po: cierto: q el estādo so la guarda de su
ama que oc:aua muchas vezes la cama, y
echauase en tierra. y dēde embiaro lo apa
lencia pa q ap:ēdiese la ciēcia: z po:q mejor
pudiese ap:ender: no beuio vino .x. anos. E
seyēdo muy grā hābre enla tierra: vendio
los libros z quāto hauia: z diolo todo alos
pobres. y creciēdo su fama de biē en mejor
fizolo canonigo regular el obispo de osma:
enla su yglesia z despues seyēdo tal como el
pejo en vida fizierōls todos p:io:. y el de no
che z de dia siēp:e o:aua: z leya: z rogaua a
dios cōtinuamēte q le diesse esta grā cō q
pudiese p:ocurar la salud ōlas animas delos
rpianos. E yēdo cō su obispo a tolosa fallo
q vn su huesped era hereje: z cōuertiolo ala
fe de jesu rp:o z p:sentolo a dios en p:micias
mas vn dia p:oicādo sctō domigo cōtra los
herejes escriuio las auto:idades: z dio las
avn hereje po:q ouiese tiēpo de responder
a ellas. y estādo aqlla o:a los herejes assen
tados al fuego mostro aqlla carta que auia
tomado: z dirierō le sus cōpaneros que la
echasse enel fuego: z si se qmase q la su fe se
ria: y era verdadera: z si no se qmase que p:e
dicariā q la fe delos rp:ianos era verdadera

CRAVING FOR SOLITUDE

God had laid hold on and transformed this soul, and remarkable things began to stir within its depths. Inigo became, in a manner, an Amadis of the ascetic life. He felt a powerful attraction to solitude, which even in the hurly-burly of a worldly career had exercised its secret appeal. In Arévalo, when he was an elegant young squire, he was once troubled by an ill-smelling nasal ulcer. In disgust the courtiers kept their distance. Inigo was seized, as he declared years afterwards, "with the urge to fly into a desert and to hide himself in an unapproachable solitude". The same urge broke out anew, but transformed into the craving to match Christ's saintly knights, of whom he had been reading, and to live on herbs like the holy hermit Onofrius in Egypt. The saint's life told how he had undertaken his struggle against "the enemy of man's nature", and how then he uttered the inspiring words: "My heart is aflame, and my spirit leaps upwards, when I leave the pleasures of this world and give myself with all my strength to God." This was now the way of Inigo. "He sought to take upon himself flagellations and fasts in the measure of a generous heart afire with the spirit of God." The solitude of the Charterhouse beckoned him. Not far away from Seville was the monastery of Cuevas, famous throughout Western Europe, sufficiently distant for Inigo to bury himself there. He had seen on more than one visit the splendid monument church of the Castilian kings at Miraflores in nearby Burgos, where austere monks lived in silence and prayer. Night after night Inigo contemplated the glitter of stars over the hills of Oñazmendi. Everywhere his soul had now one single purpose, passionate and mysterious, to be solitary with his solitary God. A house servant was despatched to Burgos, to bring back information about the rule of St Bruno. Then this longing cooled, and there came upon him the urge to wander in pilgrim guise throughout the entire world. For where was God? The wonderful page in his autobiography in which all this uncertainty is described, conceals beneath these adventurous projects that original experience of which Inigo had read in the life of St Francis of Assissi. There God said to the Poverello: "Francis, take the bitter things for sweet, and despise thyself, if thou really desirest to know me." To abandon everything in starkest poverty, to walk unknown as a pilgrim through the world, to be treated with contempt: this was what filled his mind. "He wished then to recover complete health to get ready for this journey."

THE CRAVING FOR SOLITUDE

Notes on the four plates that follow:

69 DOOR OF THE CHURCH OF THE CARTHUSIAN MONASTERY AT MIRAFLORES

The Carthusian monastery near Burgos was established by the father of Queen Isabella. The church was constructed from 1454 onwards by t he architects, John and Simon of Cologne The tympanum over the doorway contains the Pietà, to which Queen Isabella was very devoted. Above, the coat-of-arms of Castille and León (castle and lion), and the shield of the founder.

70 FUNERAL MONUMENT OF THE INFANTE DON ALONSO (DIED 1470)

The work of Gil de Siloe.

71 THE PARENTS OF QUEEN ISABELLA

The founder of the monastery, John II of Castille, and his consort Isabella of Portugal, flanked by the four Evangelists. The photograph shows St Luke with the steer. Within four years, 1489 to 1493, the same artist had completed these two masterpieces in alabaster.

72 MADONNA FEEDING CHILD

Round the funeral monument runs a garland of small statuettes: of saints, smiling infants, grotesque figures grimacing, and a tracery of tendrils.

OUR LADY'S PILGRIM

Inigo's conversion was further enriched by an interior experience which he has described with a delicate modesty: "As one night he lay awake, he saw clearly a picture of our Blessed Lady with the Holy Child Jesus." This silent vision filled him with a keen disgust of the sins of his former life and thoroughly transformed him. From now on Mary becomes the High Liege of his heart. Frequently he would salute her statue as he turned his mule up the steep pathway to the hermitage of Olaz. He wrote down her words in blue ink in the quarto volume of 300 pages where he noted passages that had impressed him in the books which had led to his change of mind and heart. Now he felt himself completely healed in body and soul. There was nothing to keep him any longer in the castle of Loyola. With overflowing gratitude he knelt before the picture of the Mother of Sorrows in the house chapel. He saw before him the way he must go; over the holy mount of Montserrat to Barcelona by the sea and thence to Jerusalem.

Martín García, who during these months had fought against France and added to the military renown of Loyola, sensed, when he returned home, something of the change which had taken place in the stern, silent Inigo. One day he conducted him through the rooms of the castle and conjured up all the bright hopes that were awaiting him. Inigo could only smile. For him this world had gone for ever. At the close of February 1522 he made a pretext of visiting the Duke of Nájera in Navarrete and accompanied by his brother priest Pero López and two attendants, he set out on horseback for Oñate, elegantly attired, to visit his sister Magdalena. At that time Guipúzcoa was the storm centre of the Spanish war policy, and in Vitoria news had just reached the Regent, Cardinal Adrian, of his election as Pope. All this, however, had no interest for Our Lady's pilgrim. On the other hand, he persuaded his brother, the companion of his nightly excesses at carnival time seven years previously, to spend the night in vigil with him at the shrine of Aránzazu, held in reverence throughout the Basque land. Here Inigo made a vow of perpetual chastity to

Our Lady. For he knew his weaknesses. Afterwards he spoke as follows to a friend: "As he left his homeland to go to Montserrat he was more afraid of being overcome by the sin of the flesh than by any other burden; it had occasioned him many a struggle and defeat. Consequently, he made a vow of Chastity to Our Blessed Lady and entreated her to take him under her protection and patronage."

In Oñate Inigo dismissed the two attendants and took leave of his brother and sister. With a happy feeling of freedom he rode down to Navarrete. He did not find the Duke there, who now needed all his time and money to stage a splendid reception in Nájera for the newly-elected Pope. But he did acquit his outstanding obligations to the hero of Pamplona with the words: "Money may be wanting for everything else, but debts to Loyola have to be paid." Inigo settled some bills that still were unpaid from his hectic period in Navarrete. The rest belonged to his new Lady. Some of it went to restore a picture of Our Lady in the parish church which had fallen into decay.

OUR LADY'S PILGRIM

Notes on the four plates that follow:

73   PILGRIM WAY TO ARÁNZAZU

On June 11th 1468, Our Lady appeared in a thorn bush, such as is seen in this photograph, to the Basque shepherd boy Rodrigo de Balzategui. In his astonishment the boy asked, "Aránzazu?", that is, "Are you under the thorns?"

74–75   "ANDRA MARI", "THE LADY MARY", FROM ARÁNZAZU

Sculpture in stone from the thirteenth century placed over the trunk of a thorn bush. Basque devotion has surrounded this miraculous figure with the splendour of silver and brocade.

76   THE MONASTERY NEAR THE SHRINE

Here Inigo came into contact with the sons of St Francis. When the monastery was burned down in 1553, Ignatius secured an indulgence for its rebuilding in grateful memory of his pilgrimage.

THE NIGHT VIGIL

Spring begins gently in the Ebro valley. At the beginning of March 1522, Inigo rode happily by Logroño and Tudela towards Catalonia, towards the adventures he was dreaming of for God. He still wore his rich clothing, but near his heart he carried his one legacy from Loyola, a little picture of the Mother of Sorrows. In the inns at night-time he disciplined himself to blood. His soul then was blind, as he declared later looking back upon these days with maturer vision, "and did not yet understand what humility was or love, and the meaning of patience and wise discernment". When near Pedrola he was seized with the wish to give a couple of pious dagger thrusts to a Moorish fellow traveller who expressed doubts of Mary's perpetual virginity. In Igualada, at the foot of Montserrat he bought: a garment of hemp-linen, a rope girdle, a pilgrim staff, a gourd, and rope sandals to protect his aching feet. This precious bundle was stuffed into a saddlebag. It was to be his new uniform at his night's vigil before Our Lady's statue. He had thought this out as a parallel to the story of Prince Esplendian in the romance of Amadis. Very soon his mule stood outside the celebrated mountain monastery. It was the 21st of March. Here Inigo intended to make a clean break with the past and to place his pilgrimage to Jerusalem under the charge of his Lady. For the next three days he examined his conscience with the help of the Confession booklets which were provided for pilgrims and handed to the pious Benedictine, Juan Chanones, a neatly prepared list of all the sins of his life. Chanones gave him a present; he was Inigo's first guide in the ways of prayer and it was from his hands that Inigo received the Spanish edition of the famous "Exercises" of Abbot Cisneros, who in recent years had brought the religious spirit of Montserrat to its highest bloom. Inigo presented his mule to the monastery, his expensive clothes he gave away secretly and by the light of evening to a poor beggar. Sword and dagger, however, were the property of the Lady of his heart, whose time-honoured image was throned in mystery behind the grill of the pilgrimage chapel. Now the vigil could begin. For the feast of the

Annunciation thousands of pilgrims had arrived. Proud in his lowliness, Inigo in his new garments approached for the first time the dark Madonna. He was unrecognised. His good sword hung on the grill as his gift of dedication. The golden lamp, a present from the Emperor Charles V, shone and sparkled, numberless candles illuminated the holy image. Inigo stood or knelt motionless, as the old knightly custom demanded. At midnight the monks chanted Matins. There was a sound of bells from the hermitages as once before at Loyola. At two o'clock commenced the pilgrims' Mass. The clear voices of the choirboys intoned: "Hail, Thou Morning Star." Inigo received with consuming love the sacramental body of his Lord, whom now he would serve for ever.

In the grey morning light the pilgrim strode down into the valley. He had become a Knight of God, as afterwards he said to one of his religious, "according to the ancient and solemn rite of a nobleman". Over his heart gleamed the morning star. In Manresa would come the sun's full daylight.

THE NIGHT VIGIL

Notes on the four plates that follow:

77 THE ASCENT TO MONTSERRAT

The "serrated mountain" rises sharply from the Catalonian plain. In the valley the river Llobregat flows from Manresa to the sea. From the ninth century pious hermits dwelt in the clefts of the mountain and in 1030 a Benedictine monastery was built on its rocky sides. There is a view across the valley and over the splendid countryside as far as the sea.

78 THE HOME OF HERMITS

High above the monastery rise massive spires of rock, among which in Inigo's time were twelve hermitages, almost impossible to reach. On the highest spire stood the hermitage of the good thief, Dismas, which our pilgrim loved to visit.

79–80 THE DARK MADONNA OF MONTSERRAT

Painted Romanesque wooden statue from the end of the eleventh century. The face and hands have been stained black by the smoke of numberless votive candles, and from a motive of pious reverence this has been left untouched. The Emperor Charles V was profoundly impressed by the mystical atmosphere of the old pilgrimage chape and the statue of Our Lady and presented it with a golden lamp.

◄ 78
79

THE MAN IN SACKCLOTH

The time had now come for Inigo to set out for Barcelona. He was anxious, however, to note down in his small quarto volume the inspirations received during the night vigil and some extracts from the book of Cisneros. He was looking for a quiet spot where he might spend a few days. His confessor drew his attention to the religious town of Manresa not far away. Inigo turned aside therefore from the pilgrim's path. Some pious ladies from Manresa, among them Agnes Pascual, who later was to be a true mother to him, made arrangements for him. On the evening of Our Lady's feast Inigo, rope sandal over his wounded foot, walked across the old bridge over the Cardoner through the narrow alleys to the hospice for the poor of Santa Lucia. These few days of repose became ten months of consolation, of spiritual anguish and mystical transformation. Manresa became the homeland of his enlightened heart. Soon the "Pilgrim", as he now styled himself, was able to move into a tiny cell in the convent of friendly Dominicans. His food he begged from door to door with a small wooden bowl, and the street urchins called after him: "Here comes the man in the old sack." Hair and fingernails were allowed to grow. He must do penance for the elegance of Arévalo. Many a time he again climbed the height of Montserrat, to pray in some cleft amid the rocks. The monks knew him and used to say: "It is the pilgrim who has become a fool for Christ's sake." Each day Inigo devoted seven hours at Manresa to prayer. He found delight in the nightly Matins of the Dominicans and the Vespers in the church of Our Lady of Seo.

It was in these weeks that he discovered what for the remainder of his life was to prove his dearest book: the *Imitation of Christ*. He made friends with the sick in the hospital and children in the streets, and soon he was known throughout the town just as "the Holy Man". Rapt in thought he wandered frequently past the Poor Clares' convent as far as the hermitage of St Paul and prayed in Our Lady's shrine at Viladordis or by the many crucifixes along the roads. But his chief delight was to bury himself in one of the thorn-choked caves that opened along the Cardoner. There it was silent, and in the distance rose up the mighty mass of Montserrat. Inigo had found his desert.

No wonder, then, that his strength gave way before these exaggerations of asceticism. It was at Manresa that his sturdy health was permanently weakened. He himself said later and quite frequently: "In this matter I had to learn by trial and error." Twice he was sick nearly to death. Pious ladies, who were given the somewhat mocking name of "Iniguas", nursed him back to health. His stomach trouble—really the beginning of that painful bilious colic from which he suffered permanently—he would dose with a handful of figs he had begged. As the rough winter came, his friends forced him to accept at least a warm overcoat of brown colour and also shoes and a cap.

To Inigo at Manresa came that experience which is the lot of all upon whom God means to outpour His spirit. The vessel of the body had to be broken.

THE MAN IN SACKCLOTH

Notes on the seven plates that follow:

81 THE COLLEGIATE CHURCH OF MANRESA, MARIA DE LA SEO

Here, at the foot of the cross, the socket of which is still preserved, Inigo made his first prayer, as he crossed the Cardoner bridge into Manresa.

82 STREET LEADING TO THE HOSPICE OF SANTA LUCIA

Inigo begged his daily bread at doors like these.

83 THE OLD CONVENT OF THE POOR CLARES

Inigo passed this regularly, on his way to his lonely spots for prayer.

84 THE PILGRIM'S BEGGING BOWL

The bowl of olive-wood, from which Inigo is said to have eaten the soup he begged, is reverently preserved by a pious family in Manresa.

85 A PROTECTION FOR THE WOUNDED FOOT

Inigo had purchased in Igualada sandals of this kind (alpargatas), common in these parts. He wore them on his way to Manresa.

86 HOUSES ABOVE CAVES

The houses of the country folk at Manresa are built above the remarkable cave formation of the bank of the Cardoner. The nearest of these houses contains Inigo's begging bowl. Not far away stands the cross Del Tort, before which Inigo offered his thanks for the vision granted him by the Cardoner.

87 OUR LADY OF VILADORDAS

Inigo used to visit this shrine of Our Lady outside the city with special affection. He was once found there by pious women in a complete collapse through exhaustion.

[32]

84

85
86 ►

Much later, when Inigo amid the exertions of his student time in Paris looked backward to the cave of Manresà, he was in the habit of calling it his blessed "primitive church". Indeed, it was here that the Pentecostal storm broke over his heart. It was not merely illness that delayed him at Manresa; nor was it the impossibility of undertaking a pilgrimage to Jerusalem in 1522. The new Pope, whose permission he required to make the pilgrimage, only arrived in Rome after a leisurely journey in August of that year. It was the grip of mystical grace he could not resist that held Inigo in Manresa. All through the high summer it had fastened upon his soul and made of Inigo "a new man with a new understanding".

The ascent to these heights was steeper than the pilgrim path to Montserrat. The first weeks in Manresa, that were still filled with the soft afterglow of his night vigil, were followed by the dark night of his soul. Overwrought nerves caused him to see even in full daylight strange shapes which loomed up for hours on end: a glistening monster like a snake with many eyes: or during severe fasts the vision, natural enough, of an appetizing dish of meat. That he could bear with. Interiorly the thought gnawed him, expressing itself in devil's speech: "How can you keep up a life like this for seventy years?" And what about his life of sin? There commenced for Inigo the hell of tortured conscience. "Like a man threading beads on a string, he reflected on sin after sin from his past." No confessor was of any avail. All taste for spiritual things vanished. A dreary void gaped around him. It availed nothing to take refuge in the rock clefts of Montserrat, into which he would creep on all fours. It was fruitless to read the Passion at midnight prayer. The whole effort of conversion suddenly appeared absurd. Then he would try to force the return of grace through an eight days' fast. In vain. Very soon he was on the brink of desperation and suicide. Like a cry from the very depths rose his appeal to the God who had deserted him: "Hasten, Lord, to my aid, for I find no salvation in men and creatures. If there were a dog I might run after to secure help, I should do it."

God gave him answer. Slowly there came into his tortured soul the comfort of grace. Suddenly it was "as though a cloak had been taken from his shoulders". Fearful yet enraptured, he questioned himself: "What is this new life, which I am now commencing?" He was like a sleeper awakening. It was the same experience of the struggle of spirits he had had at Loyola, but with a keener sensitiveness for the manner in which God acted directly upon his soul. The first consequence of this new experience was fundamental to Inigo's development. He greatly lessened his excessive severity of penance and fasting, "he again cut fingernails and hair", the first indication of that subsequent prudent balance which allowed him to return to the world from God's solitude. The grace of the Spirit streamed now over his soul. It was on the steps of the Dominican church, as the evening Angelus was pealing, that his spirit began to be raised aloft and in the imaged harmony of three wonderful organ keys he contemplated the mystery of the Trinity. Tears of joy ran down his cheeks; from now on till his life's close Inigo's eyes were to remain inflamed by this weeping before God. "The impression was so strong, that it stayed with him his whole life long, and he experienced always a deep devotion when he prayed to the Blessed Trinity." Infinitely removed from the sensebound visions of earlier days, he now apprehended in ever finer images how God created and works within the world; he beheld as from afar the humanity of Our Lord, the manner of His presence in the Blessed Sacrament, His holy mother. And all this so clearly with such sweet simplicity, so unspoilt by man's clumsy understanding, that Inigo could describe the new manner of knowledge only in these terms: "At Manresa God treated me as a schoolmaster treats a child, and I should dishonour the very majesty of God were I to doubt that God had indeed treated me thus."

The pilgrim's spirit had been now so strengthened that it could bear to face, with no help from image or imagination, the ascent to the solitude of God. This took place in September, on one of his silent walks along the banks of the Cardoner, near the cross Del Tort high above the hermitage of St Paul. Inigo has left a description of this most sublime hour of his life. "When he had walked a portion of the way, he sat down and gazed at the river. The eyes of his spirit began to open. It was not that he actually beheld some vision but rather there was given to him a knowledge and understanding of many things of the spiritual life, of faith and theology. This was accompanied by so brilliant an enlightenment that everything appeared new. Impossible to describe in detail what he then grasped. This alone can be said, that he acquired a wonderful clarity in his mind. Were he to put together all the graces of God received throughout his more than two and sixty years of life and add to this total all he had ever known, it would not in his judgment be as great as what he then experienced on that single occasion. This experience made so profound an impression on him that his spirit remained illuminated. It was as though he were transformed into another person. He threw himself down on his knees before a crucifix which stood nearby to express his gratitude to God."

This hour made of Inigo the Ignatius of the future.

What he had obscurely glimpsed at Loyola of Christ's kingdom and the battle of different spirits, shone forth now with crystal brilliancy. Inigo was overwhelmed by the discovery: this Christ is here *now*, His kingdom is being fought for in the Church, the combat of spirits continues through all ages and invades all hearts, and it is always decided by the cross of the God who became poor for our sake. We must therefore "help souls", for this King seeks men who will fight on His side, men not craven but full of love and energy. This "call of the King" was just the right appeal for the silent courage of the knight of Loyola. Hour after hour he had to reflect on it all in his cave. In his cell at the Dominican friary he wrote it down in a new notebook, briefly, clumsily, yet with the uncanny certainty of a man who had experienced the Divine itself. The book of the *Spiritual Exercises* was in the making. Many phrases from Ludolph, from the *Imitation of Christ*, and from the pious handbook of Chanones find their echoes in it. But as a unity, in project and fulfilment, it derives from Inigo alone. It is the fruit of the mystical grace received in the cave by the Cardoner. Of this, the hour of its origin, Father Nadal, who well knew the spiritual graces of Ignatius, was later to declare: "Our Lord gave him here a profound understanding of, and a vivid feeling for, Divine mysteries and for the Church. It was here that God our Lord communicated the *Spiritual*

Exercises to him, in so far as He led him to give himself completely to God's service and the weal of souls. He showed him this goal in striking manner in the meditations of the King and of the Two Standards. In these Ignatius recognized his life's purpose—that same purpose which the Society of Jesus has made its own."

This book from Manresa has helped to transform a world.

INIGO'S PRIMITIVE CHURCH

Notes on the six plates that follow:

88 THE HOLY CAVE

Only the rockwork of the ceiling of the grotto is as Inigo saw it. Since the seventeenth century the cave has been transformed into a shrine.

89 SAINT PAUL BY THE CARDONER

The priory was then occupied by the Cistercians.

90 AS IN INIGO'S TIME

This rock cave gives an impression of the cave of the penitent at his prayers.

91 FIG-TREE AND ROCK SPRING

This cavern is in the immediate neighbourhood of the cave made holy by Ignatius. Over its sun-warmed walls ripen the figs with which the hermit of Manresa used to dose his stomach cramps. He would quench his thirst at a fresh spring such as this.

92 THE SERRATED MOUNTAIN

View from the holy cave of the mountain chain which, according to popular legend, was "serrated" or given its saw-like form by the Infant Jesus. It was for Inigo the symbol of the sacrifice and elevation of his heart.

93 FAREWELL TO MANRESA

The ancient bridge across the Llobregat near Vilumara, where in February 1523 the pilgrim bade good-bye to friends who accompanied him.

93

PENNILESS TO ITALY

A new man now, Inigo departed from Manresa on February 18th. On the ancient bridge near Vilumara he bade affectionate farewell to the pious women who had truly befriended him. A wallet held the precious spoils of the *Spiritual Exercises*: on his breast was a cross of wood which he intended to take to Jerusalem. The dress that he had adopted in exchange for the sackcloth of Igualada, was itself a symbol of his transformation: he wore an unpretentious grey-brown cassock. Since the graces received by the Cardoner it had become "his firm determination that nothing will make him abandon" to help the souls of unbelievers in Jerusalem, the city of his crucified Monarch. His eyes soon saw below them the splendid city of Barcelona in its twilight haze; beyond it the sea with the ships that seemed to beckon him. There was need to hurry if this year he was going to reach a pilgrim ship at Venice. Inigo, however, was compelled to wait for twenty days in Barcelona before he could secure a passage. But it was not time lost. He came to know some men who later were to be of great assistance to him. He stayed as a guest in the modest house of Señora Pascual, begged food, as at Manresa, both for himself and the other poor, and lived a penitent's life. Occasionally he went to visit hermits not far away from the city or had long spiritual talks with Sister Antonia, the portress at the convent of the Hieronymites.

An encounter during these days was to prove of moment in Inigo's life. One day in the church of San Justo y Pastor he was sitting among the children near the choir steps, listening with face entranced to the word of God. A distinguished lady, Isabel Roser by name, looked at him with astonishment and, as she gazed, she heard in herself a voice, saying "Speak to him, speak to him". She invited the strange man to a meal and thence onwards she became a mother to Inigo, although later she was to cause the first General of the Society not a few unpleasant hours.

The thing was to find a ship's passage. But both now and throughout the journey to the East the pilgrim had one fixed principle in his head: it must cost nothing. His plan, like that of Don Quixote later, was to travel "sin blanca", without a penny. The six silver pence that remained from his begging he left disdainfully on the harbour shore. His passage money, to quote himself, was to be "Love, Faith and Hope" alone. He had secured a place on a brig, when Señora Roser advised him to sail on a larger vessel and insisted on his taking as a minimum a supply of ship's biscuits. She saved Inigo's life, for the brig foundered soon after setting sail. On March 16th 1523 Inigo's vessel set its course for Italy. On board were a few acquaintances from Montserrat. For the most part Inigo remained in the stifling wooden cabin below deck, outside the door of which, at night-time, drunken soldiers kept up their noisy revelry. After five stormy days they reached Gaeta, the doorway to Italy.

PENNILESS TO ITALY

Notes on the five plates that follow:

94 FIRST SEA VOYAGE

In the harbour of Barcelona there is this model of the caravel, *Santa Maria*, in which Columbus discovered the new world. Inigo's ship may well have been of this type.

95–96 OLD BARCELONA

A sixteenth-century engraving shows the church of Our Lady of the Sea, with its twin towers and (in the left half of the picture) the church and squat tower of San Justo y Pastor.

97 "SIN BLANCA" (WITHOUT A PENNY)

Silver pennies from the earlier years of the reign of Charles V. The first of the coins bears his image. They are from the coin collection in Barcelona.

98 THE FIRST SIGHT OF ITALY

The fisher haven of Gaeta, with a view towards the ancient castle.

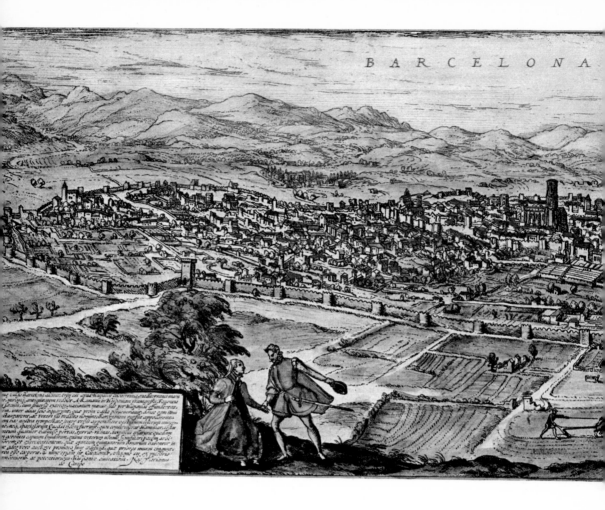

BARCELONA

95
96

97

The pilgrim stood now on the soil of Italy. Plague haunted the countryside, and there loomed the sinister threat of the Turks. On all sides the doors of inns and cities were barred and bolted; Spanish soldiery were encamped in the land. After the sea voyage Inigo was utterly exhausted, but he set out, unflinching, with his aching leg on the long journey to Rome, that would have taken an active walker full four days. During his first night's rest in a cow byre he had to protect against undisciplined soldiers two women who were travelling in his company and had been lodged in a peasant's house requisitioned by the military. For a moment he was the commanding officer once again.

When he reached Fondi, the city gates were shut. Exhausted to death, the hungry pilgrim collapsed in an open field. The next morning a happy chance brought him into touch with the mistress of the castle of Fondi, Countess Beatrice Appiani, who gave this extraordinary stranger that spoke with such courtesy, leave to rest for two days in the city. Soon Inigo's beggar's hat was again full with pennies. The journey was continued through Terracina to the Papal States, and on March 29th, Palm Sunday, 1523, passing along the ancient Via Appia, Loyola set foot for the first time in the Holy City.

It was the Rome of Pope Adrian VI, who a few months previously had arrived in Rome from Spain, though in somewhat more splendid style than the pilgrim, Inigo. It was Adrian's earnest intention to reform the city of his predecessor, Leo X, and its decadent worldly spirit. In Barcelona Inigo had discovered how people in Christendom in those days thought of Rome. When one of his lady benefactors there heard of his wish to go to Rome she was shocked and exclaimed: "What! You want to go to Rome? If you go there, heaven knows how you'll get back." Inigo found lodgings at the Spanish Hospice in the Piazza Navona and busied himself with the one thing he had at heart in the city: to obtain Papal permission for his pilgrimage to Jerusalem. Evidently he found effective help in the Vatican offices among the many Spaniards at the Curia— a large number had followed Adrian, and the Pope at this very moment was sending them home in droves. Two days after his request Inigo had the letter of safe conduct in his hands. Only a few years ago, among the dusty folios of the Vatican archives, the text of this document was discovered, which stated that "Enecus de Loyola, a cleric from Pamplona" received his pilgrimage permission on March 31st. It is the first mention of the immortal name of Loyola in the acts of the Roman Church.

No one yet knew that this poor pilgrim would be of greater significance for Papal Rome than all the attempts then undertaken by Pope Adrian to reform the Curia and to summon the Western rulers to face the danger from the Turks. Inigo had certainly heard what was then common talk in Rome. On December 21st 1522 Rhodes, the island of the Knights, had fallen into Turkish hands. On Christmas Day Sulaiman converted all its Christian churches into mosques and in the flush of victory the Janissaries were crying out: "On to Rome." Italy trembled, Hungary was on the point of collapse. The Pope was working feverishly to reconcile the Emperor with France. All was in vain. On the very day on which Inigo received his pilgrim's pass, came the French monarch's haughty refusal to the Vatican. The pilgrim must surely have pondered then on the words he had once read in Ludolph of Saxony: "Pitiful unto tears are the negligence and sloth of Christian princes who do not rescue from the unbeliever that Holy Land which Our Lord has consecrated with His blood." Loyola was arming himself for a crusade of his own special kind.

There lay another shadow athwart the Church. "On one side looms the Turk, on the other Luther threatens"—to quote from a report from these very weeks. Adrian recognized that the raging storm in Germany could no longer be contained. In the same March as Inigo, Doctor Eck, Luther's most outspoken opponent, reached Rome, and his memorandum addressed to the Pope was a desperate demand for the reform of the Roman Curia, the defects of which Adrian himself had shortly before acknowledged with brutal frankness in the Reichstag at Nuremberg. In this same spring Luther published his scandalous pamphlet against the "Papal Ass"; and the cautious and vacillating attitude of Erasmus was a great disappointment to Adrian. A few months were to pass, and on September 14th the weary Pope would lie on his death-bed: that same day Inigo prayed by the river Jordan, where once the Baptist had spoken of the axe that would be laid to the roots. Rome stood on the eve of that frightful judgment, the sack of the city. On the first tomb they prepared for the dead Pontiff in St Peter's ran the inscription: "Here lies Adrian the Sixth, whose greatest misfortune he esteemed it to be forced to rule." But in Jerusalem there knelt by the sepulchre of his humble Monarch, Inigo of Loyola, who was destined to provide a mighty succour for the Papacy.

The pilgrim had paid little notice to dying Renaissance Rome. He visited the station churches of Holy Week, prayed at the crib and cross of his Master, listened to the Easter peals of joy in St Peter's, where the first columns of the new Basilica were rising upwards between the walls of the old church. On the day after Low Sunday he started his journey North through Umbria and the Romagna. Again he was without money, in spite of the protest of his worldly-wise fellow Spaniards. The seven ducats they had pressed upon him were given away on the second day's march to beggars. Inigo was determined to be poor with the poverty of his King. During the journey the pilgrim's deathly pallor was taken as a sign of the plague. He dragged himself in sheer weariness as far as Chioggia and spent the night in an open field in front of the barricaded gates of Padua. There Christ Our Lord appeared to him in grandeur and consolation. These were days in which men went in dread and fear of plague, and it was no easy matter to make one's way to Venice. But in all these foolish circumstances of the world Inigo possessed as wholehearted a trust in the Divine help as had formerly the Poverello. Neither in Padua, city of learned doctors, did he need the requisite medical pass, nor did the inspector catch him on the boat to Venice. So he landed on the quay of San Marco in the middle of May after four full weeks of walking. His last pence sufficed for a lodging on the first night; the following evening he slept in the pillared colonnade of the Piazza of St Mark: a homeless vagabond in the rich commercial city, the stately queen of the lagoons.

SHADOWS OVER THE CHURCH

Notes on the eight plates that follow:

99   THE FIRST STEP ON ITALIAN SOIL

The Anjou fortress in Gaeta, that controls the sea. In 1503 it was conquered for Spain by the Gran Capitán, in whose army the oldest Loyola had seen service.

100   THE FIRST NIGHT'S EXPERIENCE

Near Utri, perched high on its rocks, stood the peasant's house in which Inigo had thundered against the undisciplined soldiery.

101   THE BARRICADED CITY

The Cathedral of Fondi. Here Inigo rested two days and begged the pennies for his journey.

102   THE GATEWAY TO THE PAPAL STATES

Above the rocks rise the massive foundations of the ancient Temple of Jupiter at Terracina, which formed the boundary between the kingdom of Naples and the Papal States.

103   THE ROAD TO THE ETERNAL CITY

It was along the old Roman military road of the Via Appia that the exhausted soldier of Christ approached Rome.

104–105   SHADOWS OVER THE CHURCH

As the aqueducts cast their tired evening shadows over the Campagna so there lay shadows of deep sadness across the pontificate of Adrian VI. The inscription on his monument in the German National Church expresses the tragic note of his life: "Oh, how much it matters in which periods the work even of the most excellent of men chances to fall."

106   THE HOMELESS VAGABOND

After his arrival in Venice Inigo spent his nights under the arcades of the Doge's palace.

[42]

THE LAND WHERE OUR LORD HAD STOOD

Marcantonio Trevisano, a distinguished senator, discovered the pilgrim who spent his nights under the arches of the Piazza of San Marco and looked for somewhere where he might stay. He found a refuge in the house of a wealthy fellow Basque and in that of Andrea Lippomani, the pious Prior of the former benefice of the Teutonic Knights. There was plenty of opportunity to pray and beg in Venice. In accordance with an old custom, Inigo, as a pilgrim to Jerusalem, walked side by side with a city councillor in the magnificent Corpus Christi procession on June 5th.

It was more difficult to obtain a ship's passage for the love of God from the sharp-witted ship owners of the *Serenissima*. Inigo could not, and indeed would not, produce the fifty ducats demanded by Jacobo Alberto, owner of the pilgrim ship. But he was recommended by friends to the newly elected Doge, Andrea Gritti, who saw that he was allotted a free place on the stately vessel, *Negrona*, which was to take government officials to Cyprus. News of the fall of Rhodes had caused most of that year's pilgrims to turn their steps homewards. Only thirteen brave men went aboard the pilgrim ship of Alberto, just seven sailed with Inigo on the *Negrona*. They included three fellow Spaniards, a Tyrolese, and three Swiss, among these the worthy bell-founder, Peter Füssli, from Zurich. Fussli has left us a vivid account of their adventures on the pilgrim voyage, on which Inigo himself maintained complete silence. To begin with, purchases had to be made. Biscuits, cheese and bacon, eggs and live hens, blankets and pillows, in short all the stuff that Inigo had little use for, had to be crammed into the narrow stifling cabins in the overloaded vessel.

Shortly the pilgrim flag was flying over the Piazza of San Marco, a white background with a red cross; it was the signal for departure. At this moment Inigo was lying sick with a violent fever, and the doctor told him he could embark if he wanted to be buried on the high seas. But quite undeterred Inigo went on board. On July 14th 1523 the *Negrona* weighed anchor. Vomiting during the initial sea-sickness helped Inigo half-way back to health, and from the good provender of his fellow pilgrims there was plenty over for the poor Spaniard. His true fare was confidence in God, his one comfort in those weeks of deadly heat over a languid sea was the golden glory of a mystical vision of his Master and King.

The *Negrona* needed four weeks, weeks that seemed unending, before she could anchor in the harbour of Famagusta in Cyprus. The further voyage planned, to Beirut, was not possible because of plague in Syria. The pilgrims were compelled to ride Southwards to the harbour of Salinas (Larnaca) to catch the pilgrim ship of master Alberto, which sailed on August the 19th and was not able to cast her weary anchor off Jaffa until the 31st. All the troubles of the voyage were, however, forgotten, as the pilgrims, with their escort of mischievous Turks, saw before them in the morning light of September 4th, the Holy City, Jerusalem. In silent prayer they entered the Jaffa Gate. Now Inigo could at last put into effect what once at Loyola he had noted in his conversion booklet: "With spirit afire to kiss the earth where Our Lord Himself had stood." Now began for the pilgrim the wonderful and never-to-be-forgotten experience of this happy month on the soil of Palestine: this sight of the synagogues, cities and places where God had lived as Man. Later Inigo described to his friend Favre how a consuming fire of love had thereupon seized upon him, as the Mysteries of Christ's life and passion were renewed before his living gaze, and how as a result his resolve was strengthened to remain there for his whole life. Each day the moving programme of the pilgrimage brought him new joy. On the night of Holy September 6th the pilgrims were privileged to hold a vigil in the Church of the Sepulchre and to kiss the holy spot where Christ's cross had stood. Another day they made the Way of the Cross together, reciting their prayers aloud. At the fifth station stood *"des rychen manns hus mit dem armen Lazarus"* (the rich man's house with the poor Lazarus), to quote from the travel book of the pious Swiss from Zurich. Inigo noted this too, and for a moment he may have thought of Loyola and Arévalo. He was happy now, following the poor Christ down into the waterless valley of the Kedron, past the ancient tombs, then upwards to the Mount of Olives, scene of the sweat of blood and the Ascension, where the pilgrims devoutly

[44]

kissed the footprints of the Lord. On September 8th, Our Lady's feast, they rode out to Bethlehem, first to the shepherd's cave and then to the entrance of the lovely Church of the Nativity which was walled up except for a small lower door. On September 9th Mass was celebrated at dawn in the grotto of Our Lord's birth. Inigo could not describe his happiness. "Like a poor wight and a vile bondsman" he knelt by the crib, adoring Him "who became Man for our sake". Everything became present. Christ was there. To help souls for His sake, to help these Turks who had behaved so insolently to the pilgrims on the ride to Jordan, and whose brutal Janissaries so recently had ridden down from Damascus and confined the pilgrims in their lodging for one valuable week, this is the resolution that Inigo will never let go. But how did he envisage this lay apostolate in Palestine? Probably in the same naïve way as the Poverello of Assissi when he travelled to Syria and visited the same Holy Places. The answer we find quite simply in a document from the very beginnings of the Society of Jesus: "to be ready to go to unbelievers even when nothing more could be done than to announce to them: Christ is the Redeemer."

But these were pious wishes. The guardian of Mount Sion, Angelo da Ferrara, bluntly refused him the permission to remain, and quoted the full powers conferred upon him by the Pope. That was sufficient for Inigo. To the authority of the Apostolic See he sacrificed the project of his heart without a word. But with Basque tenacity he added to himself: I shall come again, equipped very differently from now, perhaps next time not alone, myself armed maybe with full powers from the Pope. At this turning point in his life, in grim disillusionment, Inigo began to reflect for the first time on the earnest question: What am I to do now? The time for departure came. Once again, at risk of his life, he yielded to the urge to go alone to kiss the footprints of his Master as He ascended from this earth. Throughout the painful weeks of the storm-tossed journey homewards, when the pilgrims suffered from hunger and thirst beyond all measure, Inigo had time enough to meditate further on the future. When he landed in Venice in the middle of January 1524, his mind was clear. In the revelation by the Cardoner he had had a premonition, at once vivid and yet for more than a year strangely elusive, that this plan to help souls involved a search for men who, like himself, would be ready to preach Christ to unbelievers in the spirit of poverty. But companions could not be won by a vague enthusiasm for an ascetic life. Some ecclesiastical training was necessary, and for this purpose he would have to study. That was the logical and relentless consequence. Back he must go to school and to the school bench.

THE LAND WHERE OUR LORD HAD STOOD

Notes on the eight plates that follow:

107 THE BULWARK AGAINST THE TURKS

The island of Cyprus was then in the possession of the Republic of Venice. After the fall of Rhodes it was the most important bulwark against the danger from the East.

108–109 THE HOLY CITY, JERUSALEM

The view from the Mount of Olives centres on the mosque of Omar, which stands on the site of the former Temple. The two cupolas of the Church of the Holy Sepulchre are practically hidden in the maze of streets.

110 THE FIFTH STATION OF THE "VIA DOLOROSA"

The "house of the rich man", with its Gothic oriel, dates from the Middle Ages.

111 FROM THE VALLEY OF KEDRON TO THE MOUNT OF OLIVES

On September 7th the pilgrims made their way past the tombs of Zachary, James and Absalom up to Bethany and the holy places of the Ascension.

112 THE SPOT WHERE JESUS WAS BAPTIZED

Inigo visited the ford of the River Jordan on September 14th.

113 CAVES OF THE BETHLEHEM SHEPHERDS

According to pious tradition the angels here appeared to the shepherds.

114 THRESHOLD BETWEEN CROSS AND CRESCENT

The handful of Christians sought to protect themselves as best they could against the threat of the Turks. The main door of the Church of the Nativity was therefore walled up except for a low entrance. The sons of St Francis guarded the holy places in circumstances of continual danger.

[46]

114

STRAIGHT THROUGH WARRING ARMIES

In Venice the pilgrim was again a guest for two weeks in the priory of Andrea Lippomani. The example of this sensitively learned and yet sincerely mortified man showed him that it was possible to be cultured and yet poor. But Inigo was still a long way from this realization. He has himself described the somewhat ridiculous dress in which he returned from the voyage. "The pilgrim had nothing on his body except breeches of a grey stuff that came down to the knees and left his legs bare, a pair of shoes, a black cloth jacket which did not fasten properly and was badly torn at the shoulders, and in addition a short shabby cloak." His friends insisted on presenting him with a warm waistcoat and fifteen silver pieces. Inigo was still content to be the Fool of God.

Early in February 1524 he started on the never-ending tramp across Lombardy to Genoa. Arrived at Ferrara, he entered the cathedral through its magnificent door and there gave a Venetian penny to a beggar. That was enough to stir up all the poor vagabonds in the cathedral square. In a trice all Inigo's money had gone, and the delighted beggars called after him in their enthusiasm: "A saint, a saint."

Lombardy was then a seat of war. In August 1523 Pope Adrian had already constituted the League of the Emperor, England, Milan, and Genoa against the King of France, who was assaulting Italy instead of providing aid against the Turks. The Genoese Admiral Andrea Doria with his fleet was, however, on the French side. Pope Clement VII balanced anxiously between the two parties. Spanish troops of the Emperor were encamped at Milan and Pavia, the French were already on the Italian side of the Ticino near Abbiategrasso. The Spaniards were arming for an attack, and at the same time Fuenterabbia on the Basque border, which Inigo's brother had once so gallantly defended, was recaptured for the Emperor. Inigo wandered with a heavenly unconcern straight ahead through the hostile lines. The Spaniards arrested him, thinking him first of all a spy and later a harmless fool. He was beaten, but was happy none the less, contemplating Christ treated with scorn and outrage by the soldiers. He was arrested also by the French advance guard, but there he had better fortune. The officer in charge came from Bayonne and spoke good Basque. The pilgrim was allowed to go ahead without let or hindrance. In Genoa he met the Basque commandant of the prison galleys, Portundo, whom he had known in Arévalo days, and a place was found for him aboard. The crossing to Barcelona was an exciting one, since Doria was on the hunt for any Spanish caravel. But soon the towers of the chief city of Catalonia sprang into view and after a full year of pilgrim journeying Inigo disembarked safe and sound.

The time was Lent. In front of him Inigo could see the hard bench of the Latin school. But—one asks—what can deter an ardent Basque?

STRAIGHT THROUGH WARRING ARMIES

Notes on the four plates that follow:

115 MAIN DOOR OF THE CATHEDRAL AT FERRARA

Begun in 1153 in Lombard-Romanesque style. The stone in the cathedral on which Inigo knelt and prayed is still shown.

116–117 THE NEVER-ENDING ROAD THROUGH THE PO VALLEY

Roads and canals in the neighbourhood of Abbiategrasso, where Inigo came across French troops.

118 GENOA, CITY BY THE SEA

From the steep slopes of the Ligurian mountains Inigo saw once more the sea. The last stage of his pilgrim journey could now commence.

ON THE SCHOOL BENCH

In himself Inigo felt a strong attraction to return to Manresa. But a friend, a cleric with whom he purposed to study there, was meanwhile dead. He therefore established himself in Barcelona and occupied the attic in the house of Señora Pascual. Isabel Roser provided for his keep. The devout teacher, Jerónimo Ardévol, who took over the chair of Grammar at the High School in Barcelona in 1525, offered to give the elderly student some private lessons wholly free. From October 1524 onwards—having mastered the wearisome process of learning by heart words and rhymed syntax rules—Inigo was able to attend Ardévol's public school. For a man of thirty-three this was almost an heroic achievement which earned him many a prank and gibe from the boys at school with him. After two years of this, in March 1526, two examiners declared him qualified to follow lectures on philosophy in the University of Alcalà.

For the rest he lived in Barcelona also as Christ's poor fool. The dress he wore, a present from Señora Pascual, was, it is true, more clerical and, therefore, to indulge in unnoticed mortification he cut away the soles of his shoes. His heart continually found its homing way to God in burning prayers at night time, or in the sombre crypt of the cathedral. But Grammar and Mysticism were mixing badly. It was a hard decision, but Inigo gave the preference to study. During free time his one activity was to do good to souls. The back door of the Pascual house was soon beleaguered with poor folk. Inigo had a touch of genius as a beggar and soon he had won over the foremost ladies of the city to this activity. In Barcelona, "he gathered the first harvest of the *Spiritual Exercises*", and this experience helped him to give the finishing touches to his small book. The reform of the many lax convents lay near to his heart, and on one occasion this reforming zeal brought him a cudgelling from the disappointed gentlemen friends of some high-born nuns.

Meanwhile these two years in Barcelona had a particular significance for the future Ignatius—he was becoming more and more clear about the further purpose of his life. At first he had hesitated "whether after the completion of his studies he should enter some religious congregation that was in decline and disorder, in order to accept as much suffering as he could, or to retain his freedom and travel through the world on his own". But day by day it came home to him more cogently, and the radiance of Cardoner shot like lightning through the twilight of his wearisome studies; to work for souls he required companions with a disposition like his own. "Here in Barcelona arose the desire to bring together a handful of men in a fraternity, men who might be, as it were, the trumpeters of Jesus Christ." In point of fact he came across three young men, Juan de Artiaga, Lope de Cáceres, and Calisto de Sà. He gave them the *Spiritual Exercises* and made them enthusiastic for the project of going together later on to the Holy Land of Christ the King. That was the first beginning of a Society of Jesus; it came to grief, for all three later left him.

ON THE SCHOOL BENCH

Notes on the four plates that follow:

119 BARCELONA, THE ANCIENT CITY

Through this narrow Paradise Alley, Inigo was accustomed to go to the Gothic Cathedral. The Cathedral, started in 1298, was built above the crypt of St Eulalia. Inigo had a special preference for the crypt as a place of prayer.

120 "OUR LADY OF THE SEA"

This was the parish church of Inigo, constructed in the fourteenth century. The Lady Statue over the East doorway looks down upon and blesses the harbour beneath.

121 DOORWAYS OF GOD AND OF INIGO'S PATRONESS

Only a few steps divide the dark entrance to the house of the distinguished Isabel Roser from the Church of San Yusto y Pastor. It was here that this lady first met the pilgrim. Her house was always open to him as a guest and friend.

122 THE PILGRIM'S CRUCIFIX

A religious family in Barcelona still preserves the crucifix which, according to report, Inigo bequeathed to the son of his benefactress, Señora Pascual, after his return from the Holy Land.

THE GREYCOATS OF ALCALÁ

After passing his examination in Barcelona, Inigo moved to Alcalá in familiar Castille, towards the close of March 1526. His companions followed a little later. In his absurd dress the wretchedly poor pilgrim student cut a curious figure among the students of that university which had been founded by Cardinal Cisneros in 1508 and was then riding the full tide of success. The university was full of enthusiasm for Erasmus and the new culture. Inigo himself had no lofty academic aims; all he wanted "was to study for a time to prepare himself to help souls". He first repeated Latin and from October onwards attended lectures desultorily on Logic from Dominic Soto, on Natural Philosophy from Albert the Great, and a little Theology from Peter the Lombard. It was a good deal and of no great value. His sole desire, and that of his companions, was "to lead an apostolic life"; soon a fifth member joined them, Jean de Reynalde. They now made themselves long cassocks and caps of rough wool, and they were soon known in the city as the "Greycoats". Inigo lodged in Antezana hospice for the poor, the rest in private houses. The Barcelona pattern repeated itself. The poor came and went; Inigo brought them blankets, candlesticks, and anything else he could raise from friends of which he very shortly had a good number. Among these was Diego Eguia, brother of a printer, and his confessor, Father Miona—both future members of his Society. Others who subsequently became enthusiastic Jesuits regarded him at this time with real misgivings.

The working energy of this man of thirty-five years and the apostolic quality of his privileged soul prevailed over the good resolutions of the belated student. A remarkable group of religious people began to gather round him, no longer pious ladies as at Barcelona but simple folk, a baker and a wine seller, students, widows, servant girls, workers' wives and girls of doubtful character—pious and hysterical. The rumour spread about that this barefoot man in the grey smock was a noble knight from the neighbourhood of Nájera and that he had a remarkable gift for teaching a man how to examine his conscience and to pray interiorly. So they came to him, at first out of curiosity and a trifle timidly, alone or in small parties, and after such hours in the courtyard of the hospital they returned home thoughtful and affected. Some of the women went into alarming faints or were subject to attacks from the evil spirit. Without a doubt Inigo was giving the *Spiritual Exercises*, and these very mixed experiences in Alcalá taught him a lesson for the whole of his life. A secret whisper ran round the city. Were not these students "Alumbrados" in disguise, members of that ascetical sect whose underground activity was being carefully watched by the Inquisition in Toledo? Then happened what was bound to happen. In November, two gentlemen from the Supreme Tribunal of the Faith came from Toledo to Alcalá to deal with the Greycoats.

THE GREYCOATS OF ALCALÁ

Notes on the six plates that follow:

123 THE FIRST SHELTER OF THE POOR STUDENT

The home for the poor, Santa Maria la Rica, in Alcalá, in which Inigo found shelter during his first days in the city.

124–125 THE HOSPICE FOR THE POOR OF OUR LADY OF MERCY

Established in 1483 by the wealthy Luis de Antezana. Here Inigo found a permanent free shelter. He used to assemble his group of spiritual pupils in the courtyard of the hospice.

126 THE BISHOP'S PALACE IN ALCALÁ

To one side of the fourteenth-century tower the Archbishop of Toledo, Fonseca, was at that time starting to erect the new building. He was represented officially by Figueroa, the Vicar-General.

127 THE FESTIVAL ROOM OF THE ALMA MATER

This splendid room, a symbol of the humanistic culture of Alcalá in its clear Renaissance lines was completed a few years before Inigo's arrival. The Mudéjar ceiling is blended with the new style in a beautiful harmony. The modern marble tablet to the right of the pulpit includes the name of Ignatius of Loyola among its distinguished students of the sixteenth century.

128 THE COURTYARD OF THE THREE LANGUAGES

The inner courtyard of the University, which was not finished till after Inigo's student period, takes its name from the three languages—Latin, Greek, and Hebrew—to which special attention was paid at Alcalá.

123

SUSPECT OF HERESY

Now began for Ignatius an experience at once the most cruel and the most glorious of his student years; he had to pass through the prison doors of the Inquisition. On two occasions he was held prisoner in close arrest, at Alcalá and in Salamanca. A letter, written years afterwards to the King of Portugal, mentions these days behind prison bars: "God who created me and will be my judge for all eternity is my witness; for no power and for no riches on earth would I have wished to miss anything of what then happened to me."

On November 19th 1526 the commission from Toledo opened its enquiry in the episcopal palace at Alcalá. The porter of the Antezana hospice and his wife were heard as witnesses in Inigo's defence, also a Franciscan and a pious woman who every now and then had given the Greycoats some bacon or grapes or a pillow. The judges discovered nothing incriminating; and they handed the case to Figueroa, the Vicar-General, for further consideration. His decision was announced on November 21st in the name of the Archbishop: the Greycoats must at once, under pain of ecclesiastical penalty, give up their suspect habit and wear ordinary clerical dress. That mattered very little to Inigo. What he emphasised was that they had found nothing heretical in his teaching. Shortly before Christmas came some serious warnings that they must abandon secret meetings. This really was bad news for Inigo. He could not see what there was to censure in his Exercises. As far as the tribunal was concerned, the case seemed to have ended with the condition that they must have their dress dyed black or yellow.

By March 1527 a new warning reached the Vicar=General. But an examination of more women brought nothing to light. Then in the middle of April occurred a startling event. A wealthy widow with a beautiful daughter and a maid-servant disappeared without trace. They belonged to the group round Inigo; people started to scent a Greycoat mystery. On Good Friday, April 19th, a policeman knocked on Inigo's door and said, "Come along with me for a while". Without a word Inigo entered the prison and was held there for forty-two days. The interrogation on May 10th revealed an odd feminine pattern of piety and muddleheadedness. But once again there was nothing incriminating. Subsequently Inigo's arrest was made easier; he could receive friends and conduct spiritual exercises. Teresa Enríquez de Cárdenas, friend of the late Queen Isabella and a distinguished figure throughout Spain, offered him legal assistance. Inigo, however, refused all legal aid. In the meantime the missing ladies returned from their indiscreet pilgrimage and it was made clear that Inigo had advised them against it. But in an interview with the Vicar-General Inigo was compelled to listen to this sharp reprimand on the question of continuing his meetings: "I accuse you of disobedience to the commands of Holy Mother Church." Inigo could have retaliated in his own defence, but the final verdict on June 1st touched the real problem of these attempts to carry on a sort of lay apostolate. The companions were forbidden for the next three years to engage in any direction of souls "until they had pursued their studies further, for they were wanting in proper formation". This point Inigo affected most keenly when he thought it over honestly: "even though the pilgrim knew more than his companions, his knowledge lacked solid foundation."

Finally the Vicar-General made the companions a present of ordinary student dress. Inigo's changes of costume were mounting up.

Once more he was a free man, but there was no question of remaining in Alcalá. The problem arose now in even sharper outline than at Barcelona; what was to happen? A nagging discontent with the course of his studies urged him to go to the other great Spanish University, Salamanca. There he could begin over again with greater thoroughness, and the ban on spiritual direction, with which his Basque obstinacy found it hard to reconcile itself, was not binding in the diocese of Salamanca. However, he could not overcome his hesitation, and about June 21st he made up his mind to travel to Valladolid, where Fonseca, the Primate of Spain, was residing, and where he had just baptized the newly-born heir to the Spanish Crown, Prince Philip. With filial loyalty he put the decision in the hands of this prince of the Church. The Archbishop encouraged him to attend the University of Salamanca. He must decide at once for it was near the close of the academic year.

Inigo arrived in Salamanca on July 10th. The companions had preceded him and this time they lodged together. Events now took a course that was the exact opposite of his experience in Manresa. The years of peaceful study which he had planned shrank to a mere two months, and of these Inigo was again in prison for three weeks. The poor student had walked straight into a season of theological fever heat, of violent argument for and against Erasmus, and at that moment the Inquisition was holding a session in Salamanca to deal with the dangers of Northern Humanism. Inigo was soon well known in the city by professors and distinguished ladies, and frequent mention was made of "these truly apostolic men". Inigo went regularly to confession in the Dominican convent of St Stephen, a fortress in the struggle for the purity of the faith. Events moved swiftly. One Sunday the sub-Prior, Nicholas, invited Inigo and Calisto to dinner, and afterwards conducted a searching investigation in scholastic syllogisms, with which Inigo's mind—simple for all its spiritual illumination—could not deal. Suspect, he had to remain in the convent for three days, the learned friars visited him in his cell, and their opinions were divided: was this man a mystic or a heretic? Those were days when men had to walk warily —and shortly Inigo was again in prison, for twenty-two days, this time chained to Calisto. Friends in the city did all they could for him and one day he was visited by the learned Don Francisco de Mendoza, later a Cardinal in Rome and Inigo's firm friend. When the Cardinal expressed his sympathy the prisoner answered with the famous sentence: "In the whole of Salamanca there are not so many footchains and handcuffs that I would not ask for more for God's love." The volume of the *Spiritual Exercises* was examined in detail and the verdict was similar to that of Alcalá: there was nothing heretical in the teaching and behaviour of the companions, but on account of the difficulties of guidance in moral theology they must study four more years. Once again, study, study; once more the old question: what are we to do now? This problem never left Inigo's mind. The verdict had taken from him all freedom for spiritual work in Salamanca; where could he combine this freedom with properly co-ordinated study?

SUSPECT OF HERESY

Notes on the six plates that follow:

129 THE UNIVERSITY OF SALAMANCA

The main entrance of the University, regarded as a masterpiece of the so-called plateresque style. The influence of the Italian Renaissance and traditional Spanish elements from the late Gothic are here fused in a manner characteristic of the finest period of the country.

130 THE DOMINICAN CLOISTER

Inigo was examined concerning his teaching in the convent of St Stephen. The late Gothic cloister, known as "the royal cloister" on account of its magnificence, was practically finished about that period.

131 PILGRIM BEHIND BARS

Inigo was twice arrested by the Inquisition. The barred window recalls the fetters and hand-cuffs of Salamanca.

132 INSIDE THE DOMINICAN PRIORY

Inigo had to remain here for several days as an enforced guest and on his way from the refectory with the friars would have walked along this corridor.

133 THE HARD SCHOOL BENCHES

A lecture hall from the University, dating from the sixteenth century, with the lecture pulpit of Fray Luis de León.

134 STONES THAT SOAR TO HEAVEN

In Inigo's time the columns of the new Cathedral of Salamanca, that was commenced in 1513, were rising heavenwards. The pilgrim's own building plans are not yet complete.

THE MASTER OF PARIS

"Accordingly he resolved to go to Paris and study." With these restrained words Inigo announced the decision that was to guide his life into new channels. "He was led by gentle pressure towards a goal of which he was himself not yet aware," to quote from his later confidant, Nadal. He had started to think about this when imprisoned at Salamanca. How once for all to escape from the confusion that had attended his studies? That for a Loyola meant the choice of the best University in Western Europe, namely Paris. To help souls? Certainly. But from now on with the strictly limited objective of winning new companions in Paris, where was gathered the fine flower of Europe's youth. In the middle of September 1527 Inigo bade farewell to Salamanca.

His intention was to go to Paris in advance to test the possibilities of study for his companions. He loaded his books on his donkey and journeyed to Barcelona where for three months he stayed with old friends. Inigo the pilgrim was quietly yet continually developing into a man of keen worldly insight. He accepted from some pious ladies a draft for twenty-five ducats; he would require as much as that for a year's study in Paris. In the New Year of 1528 he took affectionate leave of friends and travelled alone and on foot towards Paris—to meet his Society of the future. He arrived on February 2nd.

With its four thousand students and more than fifty colleges the University was still the academic stronghold of the West, despite all the attacks of humanists and innovators. Inigo may have felt quite bewildered in the seething student life of the great city with its 300,000 inhabitants. But that was what he wanted: "here he had no temptation to fritter away his time in spiritual conversations because of his ignorance of the language and he could make better progress in his studies." A room was soon found; his Spanish room-mate squandered the ducats with which Inigo had entrusted him, so that at Easter he was once again a beggar on the streets and had to seek refuge in the pilgrim hospice of St James.

It is characteristic of his unflinching determination that on the school benches in Paris he once more started to study Latin. "Previously he had hurried too quickly from grammar to higher studies. In Paris he worked out his plan of study in a more deliberate way." This man, thirty-seven years of age, brushed up his knowledge of languages till the autumn of 1529 in the Collège Montaigu, where boys of nine were also learning Latin; he submitted himself to the severe discipline of the house, of which Erasmus once made a grim caricature, all this with the purpose of starting the full course of philosophy on the feast of St Rémy, October 1st 1529. The progress he hoped for was delayed throughout 1528 by his begging and by the long daily journey from the hospice to the college. In Paris he learnt to his cost what he later carefully recognized as Founder of the Society: that studies demand a certain security of earthly goods. In vain his Carthusian friends tried to find him a place as servant to some rich student. Early in 1529 he was advised by a Spanish monk to beg alms from the wealthy Spanish merchants in Flanders. Inigo went as far as Bruges during Lent and there found understanding and practical help from the merchant, Gonzalo de Aguilera. But in the house of Luis Vives, the famous humanist, he came across the cool sceptical spirit of Erasmus, the very thing he had been suspected of in Alcalá. This stirred all the more sensitively in him the note "of feeling with the Church" which received its final expression in the book of the *Spiritual Exercises* as a result of his studies and experiences at Paris. Inigo discovered a generous benefactor at Antwerp in the person of the Spaniard, Juan de Cuéllar, whom he visited again in the summer of 1530 and 1531: in the second of these two years he even crossed to London "from which he brought back more alms than all he had raised in these previous years". To spare him more of these begging journeys Cuéllar started to send him every year a bank draft on Paris. From 1531 onwards, Inigo was therefore assured of money, and he was able, in a discreet way of his own, to render very welcome assistance to many a poor student.

On October 1st 1529 he entered the Collège de St Barbe as a paying student. It was directed by the Portuguese, Diogo de Gouvea, and was well known for strict discipline, for its ecclesiastical spirit as opposed to the innovations of the humanists, and for the quality of its professors. His dress from now on was the student gown, the style of which he retained for the rest of his life. His room was in the top storey of the tower built on to the college and the dwelling of Master Juan de Peña, under whose direction he was now to study Scholastic Philosophy. In the same room he met two fellow students: Pierre Favre and a nobleman from Navarre, Francisco de Jassu y Xavier. Also resident in St Barbe since 1527 was a young noble scholar, Simon Rodrigues. Favre had the task allotted to him by Master Peña of teaching the rules of scholastic Logic to this student who had come late to learning. Inigo took it all with the greatest seriousness, and denied himself every escape in prayer and spiritual conversation. Aristotle had become more important than mysticism. At the beginning of 1532 he passed the regular baccalaureate examination. This was the occasion on which the students were matriculated, and it was here in the official documents of the University Rectorate that Inigo first appeared under the name "Ignatius of Loyola". Paris transformed him from Inigo to Ignatius. On March 13th 1533, after a stiff examination, he was solemnly promoted to the Licentiate of Philosophy in the Calvary Chapel of Sainte Geneviève. This gave him the right to receive the title of Master of Philosophy in a further public ceremony. However, as this involved a considerable outlay, Inigo postponed the ceremony until March 1535. Then came his great academic day in Paris. After an introductory address his name was entered on the matriculation roll of the University by the Rector, Jacquart, and a parchment, signed and sealed, was handed to him in the Church of the Mathurins to this effect: "Our dear and worthy Master Ignatius de Loyola from the diocese of Pamplona has passed searching examinations and merited the degree of Master in the world-famed Faculty of Arts of Paris with distinction and honour. In witness whereto we have affixed our great seal to this parchment." His first purpose was now achieved. Men were to address him as Master Ignatius to the end.

Meanwhile, he had not lost sight of his other purpose: to win new comrades. For the Salamanca brethren had proved unfaithful and had found their way into the world or into ecclesiastical office. In Paris he had to start over again with more circumspection. "He kept his eyes open to gain for his purpose a handful of men who appeared specially gifted and suitable." He succeeded in awakening the enthusiasm of three Spanish students, Juan de Castro, Pedro de Peralta, and the young Amador de Elduayen, for the ideals of Poverty and the Cross. Returning from his first begging journey in Flanders, he gave these three the *Spiritual Exercises*; they joyfully handed over what they possessed to the poor and entered the pilgrim hospice of St James. The excitement in the Spanish colony knew no bounds. Gouvea the Rector of Sainte Barbe threatened Ignatius with a public flogging on the grounds that he had turned little Amador into "a madman". Doctor Ortiz of the Collège Montaigu denounced him to the Inquisitor in the Dominican convent. In these days of excitement Ignatius had been absent from Paris. The student who had squandered his original ducats was lying sick to death in Rouen. Ignatius made a forced march of three days to Rouen to assist him, with no provisions for the journey—it was on this occasion that he experienced an uncontrollable flood of spiritual joy as he hastened over the hills of Argenteuil. He returned to find his comrades the centre of disturbance and at once and without a summons presented himself before the Inquisition. The danger passed, but "this second birth", as it was called with a smile, was again a miscarriage: Castro became a Carthusian in Spain, and Peralta a wealthy canon of Toledo: of Amador's subsequent career we know nothing.

His friendship with the room-mates at Sainte Barbe was meanwhile growing fast. He was led into spiritual conversations with the thoughtful Savoyard Favre in spite of Aristotle—an exercise that ran counter to his resolve "not to seek any more for companions, in order to pursue study quite undisturbed". After the spring of 1531 Favre was won over. But he had much more difficulty with the young gentleman from Navarre. An opinion later attributed to St Ignatius was that the most intractable material he ever had to handle was Francisco de Xavier. The elderly student calmly put up with the clever mockery of his elegant and intelligent room-mate, helped him financially, found pupils for him to tutor, and warned him of the dangers of Humanism. In 1533 Xavier also had been completely won over and for ever. At the same time Ignatius paid much attention to Rodrigues the Portuguese, and at the end of April 1532 he happened to meet two Spanish students who had already heard of this extraordinary Inigo at Alcalá, Diego Laynez and Alfonso Salmerón. And when another Spaniard, the bluff and genial Nicholás Bobadilla, in his rough friendly way, turned to Ignatius, well known for the help he gave to students, Ignatius realised that he had round him a group of young men in whom his keen insight could detect just the right qualities for "the new life". This time his project would succeed.

After his Licentiate Ignatius began the study of scholastic Theology with the Dominicans of Saint-Jacques, in whose college St Thomas had once lectured. All his life long he remained attached to the teaching of Aquinas. But in addition, ever since those days by the Cardoner he possessed a knowledge which made a Doctor of Theology in Paris remark on one occasion: "I have never heard any single man speak on theological matters with such a mastery and reverence."

It was this above all that the new companions were to realise. The room in the tower of Sainte Barbe became their souls' true home. Beginning in January 1534, Ignatius took them one by one through the *Spiritual Exercises*, Francis Xavier being the last of them in September. Then with prayer and austere practices they strengthened themselves in the resolution "to adopt the way of life of Ignatius", or, as Laynez later put it, "to abandon the world completely and to dedicate themselves to the way of Poverty and the Cross". That was the high purpose of the *Spiritual Exercises*. Sunday after Sunday the comrades received Communion together in the Carthusian monastery. By dint of spiritual conversation and friendly mutual visits these seven men grew soon into a genuine community of one single mind and heart.

THE MASTER OF PARIS

Notes on the eight plates that follow:

135 THE HEART OF PARIS

Ignatius's daily journey from the pilgrim hospice to the Collège Montaigu led him past Notre Dame in Paris. He may frequently have meditated on the mysteries of Our Lady's life which appear in the arch over this main door.

136 PARIS IN THE MIDDLE AGES

Little remains today of the Paris of Ignatius's time. To the West of the student quarter stands the Romanesque church of Saint Germain-des-Prés. A solitary pathway used to lead from this church to the Carthusian monastery where Ignatius and his friends were in the habit of hearing Sunday Mass.

137 THE LATIN QUARTER

The college buildings of Sainte Barbe and Montaigu, where Ignatius studied, have long since disappeared. This old print conserves the impression that would have been made in the sixteenth century by the Sorbonne, seat of the world-famous Faculty of Theology of Paris.

138 KNOWLEDGE AND WISDOM

In taking his companions through the *Spiritual Exercises* Ignatius not only emphasised the pious reading of the *Imitation of Christ* (an edition of 1554 is shown in the photograph) but also the thorough study of Scholastic Theology. One example of their keenness in this second matter is this well-stocked notebook of extracts from the Scriptures and the Fathers of the Church. It belonged to Bobadilla and has the inscription: "to God's honour and the welfare of souls, anno 1534."

139 THE CHURCH OF THE FACULTY OF ARTS

The Faculty of Philosophy held its solemn meetings and elected the Rector of the University in the Church of St. Julien-le-Pauvre, dating from the twelfth century.

140 THE PILGRIM'S EXULTANT PATHWAY ACROSS THE FIELDS

This is Ignatius's description of the mystical experience which occurred on the hill of Cormeilles-en-Parisis. The old windmill still stands on the spot.

141 MEETING WITH LUIS VIVES IN BRUGES

A contemporary engraving of the famous humanist (1492–1540). The inscription praises him as a light of Europe that shone from his home in Valencia to the far Flemish North.

142 THE MASTER OF PARIS

The Roman Archives of the Society of Jesus contain this original document, made out on March 14th, 1535, in the name of Ignatius of Loyola.

135 ▷

LVDOVICVS VIVES VALENTINVS

Splenduit in terra gelidam quæ reſpicit Arcton
Natum fœlici ſydus in Heſperia:
Fllius ac totum radij effulſere per Orbem
Viues doctrina & quos tulit & pietas.

B

12

142

THE VOW AT MONTMARTRE

The companions now desired to seal this community of theirs with a sacred vow. Lively debates were held; they were determined after the conclusion of their studies at the beginning of 1537 to serve God in complete poverty, to make a vow of chastity, and to travel to the Holy Land. Ignatius and Xavier proposed to remain there permanently, but they encountered opposition. Prudently, Ignatius added some conditions to the vow: should the voyage prove impossible within the space of a year, or if they were unable to remain permanently in Palestine, or supposing that the majority decided it would be better to return to Europe, their plan was to place themselves at the disposal of the Holy Father in Rome "that Christ might deign to show them through the mediation of His Vicar upon earth what was the way of His greater service".

On the feast of the Assumption, August 15th 1534, the seven comrades made their way out of the city to the chapel of the Martyrs on the slopes of Montmartre. Favre, recently ordained priest, said Mass in the dark crypt, and they all recited their vow formula before receiving Communion. It was a day of radiant happiness. Decades afterwards Bobadilla could recall this hour: "I remember how at Montmartre in Paris on this feast-day we, the first Fathers of the Society, made the vow to go on pilgrimage to Jerusalem and how Divine Providence, that deep abyss of wisdom, transformed that vow to a finer 'pilgrimage' which led to the foundation of a religious Order. By God's grace the Society has expanded throughout the world and daily I see it develop for His greater glory. Praised be Jesus Christ."

About this time the old gall trouble was causing Ignatius frequent and protracted pain, and doctors and his companions both insisted that for his health's sake he should pay a visit to his Basque country. At the beginning of April 1535, Ignatius yielded to this pressure and to ease the journey the brethren bought him a small horse. He committed his new company to the charge of the ever-faithful Favre, who during the next two years won three more Frenchmen for the company, Claude le Jay, Paschase Broët, and Jean Codure. Twice they met in the Montmartre Chapel of the Assumption to renew their vows. Their intention was to rejoin Ignatius again in Venice at the commencement of 1537 to enter upon the pilgrimage of their vow.

The years of study in Paris and the high festival of Montmartre were of decisive significance for Ignatius and his future mission. Not that this future Society was already in existence. But their grounding in the theology of Aquinas and the strength they now derived from their vow were directing himself and his comrades along that pathway which the graces of Manresa had already foreshadowed: towards the Church, that was made visible there in the person of Christ's Vicar upon earth.

THE VOW AT MONTMARTRE

Notes on the four plates that follow:

143 OUTSIDE THE CITY WALLS

This section of the map of Paris for 1551 shows the way taken by the companions on August 15th 1534 from the Montmartre gate through vineyards to the Chapel of the Martyrs.

144 THE HILL OF MARTYRS

This Pietà, originally from Saint Germain-des-Près and now in the Louvre, was painted by a Rhenish master in 1410. The background is a picture of old Paris with Saint Germain-des-Près, the Louvre, and Montmartre. On the summit is the old Abbey Church, on the slopes the Martyrs' Chapel.

145 AUGUST 15TH 1534

This engraving from the first biography of Ignatius with illustrations, published at Antwerp in 1610, purports to represent the actual moment of the vows. It is historically incorrect as to the number and age of the companions.

146 FAREWELL TO PARIS

Late Gothic porch at Saint Germain-l'Auxerrois. From Paris Ignatius received his theological grounding in the spirit of Aquinas, in which the Gothic Middle Ages have been crystallised into a permanent form. In 1537, when in Venice, he was sent a document attesting his blameless purity of faith by the Dominicans of Saint Jacques.

143 ▷

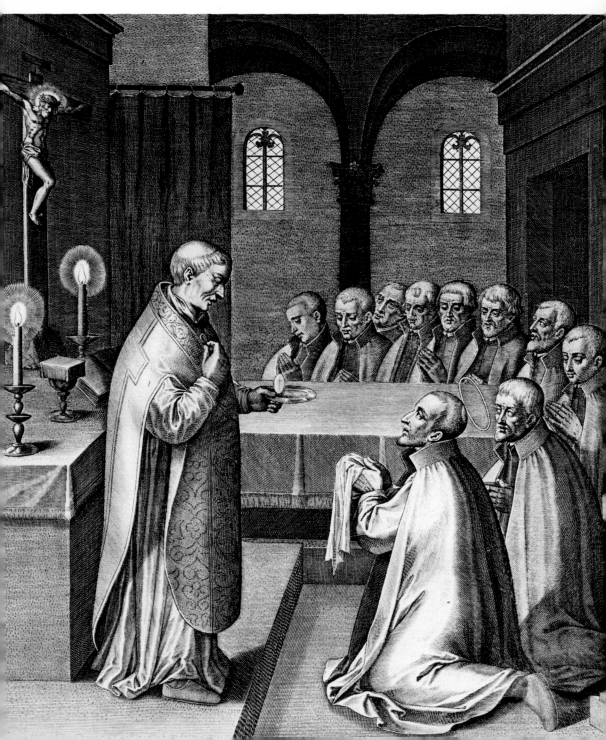

From Paris Inigo rode on his brown steed Southwards through France for fully three weeks. And as he rode he put all his plans to rights. It was not really the hope of recovered health that took him for the last time to his own country. At this precise moment when the future had been settled in Paris, he desired in the first place to make amends in Azpeitia for the scandals of his youth, to show himself with a clear countenance in the Spain that had persecuted him, to pay a visit of comfort to his companions' families, and, if possible, to regain his lost friends of Alcalá. At Bayonne he was recognised despite his pilgrim costume and rope slippers, and the report of his coming hastened before him to Loyola. Inigo rode by lonely sidetracks over the mountain ridge of Andatza to the inn at Iturrioz. His brother's two envoys were there to meet him, and a playmate of bygone days recognised him through a chink in the room door. It was all over with the ascetic incognito of his homecoming. On one point, however, he was adamant. He obstinately refused to live in the ancestral house, and chose for his lodging the hospice for the poor near the hermitage of St Magdalena. To his incensed brother he at once made the meaning of his visit clear: "I have not come to live in a castle but to sow the word of God, and to make the people realise how terrible a thing is mortal sin."

A splendid hour had struck for the inmates of the hospice. Everything that this Loyola received by begging at the doors in Azpeitia appeared on their table, and the former Lord's son was happy to eat with them. The master from Paris then started his apostolic work, with greater maturity and deliberation than at Barcelona and Alcalá; now, in fact, he was the future Ignatius of Rome. First he collected the children for catechism; he had a genius for teaching this in Basque. Soon, behind the children, a ring of adults gathered; even Don Martín García would be present, listening with a blend of shame and bewilderment. There was a constant going to and fro in his small room, persons in despair or at loggerheads, and the spiritually sick found comfort with him. Then he began to preach. He spoke of mortal sin like a man having power, his words thundered far afield. The grass in front of the hermitage was trodden bare by the feet of unnumbered listeners. He used to climb a plum tree near the hermitage at Elosiaga to give the people a better chance of following him. On one occasion he stood in the parish pulpit at Azpeitia and, his eyes turned to the font where he had been baptized, preached an inspiring sermon on the mystery of the Trinity—from the very pulpit of his sinful brother who had died truly penitent six years previously. There was almost a riot in city and countryside; they had never known a Loyola behave like this. Witnesses told how "like a bishop" he attacked the corrupt manners of the clergy; their concubines, who behaved as though they were regularly married women, were mercilessly called to order. By means of an agreement, solemnly signed, Inigo settled a scandalous quarrel between the local clergy and the convent of poor Franciscan nuns. For the rest his pastoral methods had grown in skill and prudence and he took care not to be carried away by a first flush of enthusiasm; here again he was the Ignatius of the future. Coolheadedly he collaborated with the mayor and with his brother, the church patron, to improve local morals by means of public regulations. These dealt with gambling and with begging abuses: it was curious that it should be Inigo, the beggar of Christ, who drew up the well-considered plan to regulate the poor in his home town. And to make sure that his homeland should not forget the enormity of mortal sin he renounced the remnant of his inheritance so that his brother, with the entailed estate, might make an endowment to the Church. Every day at noon the bells of the parish church and the hermitages were to be rung as a warning to those in mortal sin. In spite of a severe bout of sickness during his last weeks there, Inigo could note with contentment: "With the help of God he harvested rich fruit."

There remained his own family. In the manor house of Loyola the old sin, with which Inigo had been familiar, was still rampant. When his sister-in-law Magdalena implored him amid tears to spend at least one night in the castle, Inigo grasped the situation. One night at the rear door of the building he caught a loose woman sneaking into the castle to her paramour, locked her in his room for the night, and that was the end of the Loyola scandal. On the same day,

[66]

July 23rd 1535, Inigo put his signature to a document which settled the question of his sister Magdalena's inheritance. He then prepared to leave. At the close of July, at the frontier of the Basque land, near Puerto de Echegárate, he bade farewell to brother and home for the last time.

His heart always retained its loyalty to the Basque country and later, in a letter to Azpeitia, he saluted "this soil on which God in His mercy gave me my ancestry and my bodily existence".

He walked past the walls of Pamplona, for him so fraught with destiny, as far as Obanos, and there handed to the Captain, Juan de Azpilcueta, a precious epistle from his brother Francisco de Xavier. He next descended to Castille, glowing in summer heat, to visit the family of Laynez at Almazán, and on to Toledo to the homely parents of the young Salmerón. In Madrid he saw the eight-year-old prince, Philip, and then crossed Spain to Valencia. Here he hoped to secure a sea passage, and in the meantime he was free to pray to his heart's delight and to assist souls. Even here some unpleasant gossip was current about the supposed "secrets of Inigo", as was hinted years subsequently by the holy Archbishop Thomas of Villanueva. The Holy Grail of the Last Supper was venerated in the Cathedral here, and in its presence all the happiness he had experienced in the Holy Land flooded back to life. Shortly he would be returning there for good. He passed eight days of bliss and mystical converse in the Carthusian monastery near Segorbe with his friend Juan de Castro. Thus was his farewell to Spain blessed by God.

During the crossing to Genoa the ship ran into a terrible tempest and nearly foundered. But the pilgrim's soul, faced with the threat of death, was filled with a lofty calm, save for the one regret common to saints that he had not made fuller use of the graces given him by God. At one moment of his journey over the Apennines he saved his life by scrambling along on all fours; "it was", he declared, "the greatest physical exertion he had ever made". Arriving at Bologna he tumbled into the slimy moat round the walls and then lay sick in the Spanish hospice. Nevertheless in spite of all these hazards he arrived in Venice at the beginning of 1536 and devoted another year to quiet study.

On January 8th 1537 he was able to embrace "his nine friends in Our Lord, the comrades from Paris". They had been compelled to leave earlier owing to the renewal of hostilities between the Emperor and the French King. They had departed from Paris on November 15th 1536, and made their way across Lorraine and Northern Switzerland, crossed the snow-clad Alps of Tyrol, and, as Favre remarked in his diary, were re-united with their beloved Inigo in Venice "in good health and the happiest of spirits".

Their great adventure, their pilgrimage to Jerusalem, could now begin.

PREACHING TO HIS OWN FOLK

Notes on the eight plates that follow:

147 THE VALLEY OF HIS YOUTH

This is the view Inigo had of his homeland when he returned from Paris for his last visit.

148–149 THE HOSPICE FOR THE POOR OF ST MAGDALENA

The last of these houses along the river Urola was Inigo's dwelling in preference to his ancestral castle. There was a view of the mountain slopes through the old Gothic window of his room.   It was here the people flocked for Inigo's sermons.

150–151 OVER THE HIGH PLATEAU OF CASTILLE

Inigo trudged wearily and for the last time across Castille in its summer heat . . . a journey he had so frequently made on horseback.

152–153 THE HOLY GRAIL

The "Holy Grail" was venerated in the chapter room of the Cathedral at Valencia, a work of finest fifteenth-century Gothic. The bowl of the chalice is an ancient sardonyx, to which the foot and handles were added in the Middle Ages. Inigo, who had shown such reverence for the relics of Our Lord in Palestine, such as the pillar of the scourging and the footprints of the Ascension, would certainly have prayed here.

154 THE CARTHUSIAN MONASTERY "VAL DE CHRISTO"

Not far from Segorbe was the Carthusian monastery, today half in ruins, in which Inigo passed his last days on Spanish soil with his friend, Juan de Castro.

[68]

154

ORDINATION AMID WAR'S ALARMS

The interval till July, when the pilgrim vessels were accustomed to set sail, was fully employed. Master Inigo was an inexorable master on the "way of Poverty and the Cross". He immediately divided his ten companions—the Spaniard Diego Hozes had joined them in the past year—between two city hospitals, that of Giovanni e Paolo and the Giudecca which contained the "incurables", victims of the appalling French disease. By mid-March it was time to go to Rome to ask for the pilgrims' blessing from the Pope after Holy Week. For reasons of prudence Inigo remained behind in Venice. On Easter Tuesday the "masters" were afforded the opportunity of an academic dispute in the presence of Pope Paul III in the Castle of St Angelo and they were privileged to receive not only a blessing for the pilgrimage but also permission to be ordained priests. They had been given a money draft of 260 ducats as alms for the journey, and so they returned to Venice at the beginning of May delighted with their success.

In this very month of May Suleiman was fitting out a gigantic fleet at the Golden Horn in order to threaten Italy by attacking the Imperial power of the West. At first Venice preserved an anxious neutrality, but from July onwards it proved impossible to avoid clashes with the Turkish ships in the Sea of Ionia. For the first time in thirty-eight years no pilgrim ship left the harbour— Divine Providence conducts politics in its own way. Amidst these battle alarms the sublime day of ordination arrived for Ignatius and his friends. They placed their vows of poverty and chastity in the hands of Veralli, the Papal Nuncio, and on June 24th they were ordained priests by Bishop Nigusanti of Arbe.

A slender hope of a passage still remained, but it was decided that they should, for the time being, separate to a few cities in the Venetian Republic with the purpose of preparing for their first Masses by three months of solitary prayer: after the first fortnight, however, they would begin preaching in the open streets. On July 25th Inigo went with Favre and Laynez to Vicenza, where they found a refuge completely to their taste in the half-ruined monastery of San Pietro in Vivarola just outside the town ramparts.

ORDINATION AMID WAR'S ALARMS
Notes on the eight plates that follow:

155   SICK IN BOLOGNA
Interior courtyard of the Spanish College at Bologna which had been completed by the time of Ignatius. Inigo had hoped to continue his studies here, but after seven days of sickness the Lombardy fog made him seek refuge in Venice.

156   SERVING THE SICK IN WEALTHY VENICE
The square in front of the Scuola San Marco, a club for distinguished Venetians. Next to it stands the church of Giovanni e Paolo behind which in Inigo's time lay the hospital in which some of his comrades nursed the sick.

157   A GUEST AT THE BENEFICE OF THE TEUTONIC KNIGHTS
A century after Inigo's residence in Venice, the Baroque church of Maria della Salute was constructed on the site of the former benefice of the Teutonic Knights. On the opposite bank of the Grand Canal is the palace of the Doge Gritti with the picture of the Madonna.

158   CATHEDRAL OF ST MARK
It was in 1536, at this very period, that Sansovino began to build the splendid old Library on the right side of the harbour square.

159   WAR COMRADES
A fourth-century group of sculpture in porphyry near St Mark's. Inigo's comrades were linked as brothers in a crusade without military weapons.

160   THE BEGGAR AT PALACE DOORS
Inigo commenced his apostolate of the streets in Vicenza as the poor man of Christ. The Contrada Porti, with palaces from the fifteenth century.

161   THE TUMBLEDOWN MONASTERY
The miserable house of San Pietro in Vivarolo near the gates of Verona was taken down in 1815. This farmhouse stands in the immediate neighbourhood.

162   VISITING THE SICK IN BASSANO
At the close of August 1537 Inigo, though sick with fever, walked a full day's journey from Vicenza to Bassano, where his companion Rodrigues lay gravely ill in a hermitage on the nearer side of this bridge over the Brenta.

I WILL BE FAVOURABLE TO YOU IN ROME

This was the last occasion in the pilgrim's life on which he discovered the solitude for which he had once so strongly craved. All the springs of the graces of Manresa welled up in him again. He scarcely noticed fever and hunger, was happy to beg dry bread at the palace doors in Vicenza, and from it he prepared a mash for his friends in the monastery ruins. In September he started to preach in the streets. A wave of his hat collected an astounded audience that he addressed in a precious mixture of French and Latin which he imagined was Italian. His first Italian sermon began with these words: "Hojourdi Sancta Mater Ecclesia."

In the meantime open hostilities had broken out between Venice and the Turks, and on September 13th 1537 the Doge Gritti joined the League of the Emperor and Pope. A pilgrim passage was completely out of the question. In consequence Inigo summoned all the comrades to Vicenza for the end of September to discuss the new situation. These October talks in Vivarolo were of great significance for the Society of Jesus that was to be. The little company stood at the crossroads. Their basic plan remained always the same: to travel to the Holy Land as they had vowed to do in Montmartre. They reckoned the year of waiting, which they had anticipated, from the date in April on which they had received permission for the pilgrimage from the Pope, from Easter, 1537 until the summer of 1538. Then the second possibility included in their vow would come into force, to wit, that, in the event of a further postponement of the pilgrimage, they were to place themselves in full obedience at the Pope's disposal. For the moment there existed a political hope that, after the defeat they had suffered in September, the Turks would be ready to conclude peace, and so next year the voyage on which they were determined and for which they longed might at last commence. Accordingly Inigo postponed his first Mass which the companions had celebrated at the close of September in the monastery church at Vivarolo: he wanted to celebrate for the first time at the altar of the Nativity in Bethlehem.

The master then switched the discussion to the question: what were they to do during the interval in keeping with that ideal of apostolic work in which all were firmly united? Inigo had already a matured plan. They should no longer dissipate their enthusiasm and energies in casual preaching in the streets. Consequently he despatched his "masters" to a number of important Italian cities, Padua, Ferrara, Bologna, and Sienna. They were to try, according to circumstances, to win new recruits among the student body and engage in regular pastoral work by means of preaching, the *Spiritual Exercises*, and service in hospitals. Favre and Laynez had already received an important summons to Rome. Inigo decided to go with them to the Papal city.

These weeks of intimate association in Vivarolo gave the "masters" a sense of much closer cohesion than they had felt in Paris, where under pressure of suspicion and in reply to curious questions about the meaning of their new manner of life they had made use of the term "Company". Now on the point of separating for new labours, they searched for the most suitable title for their union. "They counselled together, what they ought to answer to the query, what sort of congregation their union was. First they prayed earnestly and then reflected what name would suit them best. And because they had no other head and no other superior than Jesus Christ, whom alone they desired to serve, they thought it best to adopt the name of their head and call themselves the 'company of Jesus'." The decision they then made marks the first point in the history of an order.

Inigo's feeling of responsibility for this developing society was now clearly shown, as it formerly had been in Paris. He insisted therefore that the unpleasant suspicions which had attached themselves to his person and teaching in Venice since 1536 should be cleared up in a judicial process. On October 13th he travelled once more to the city in the lagoons, where he was given this official testimonial: "We bear witness that Father Ignatius has led a good and holy life as a priest, that his teaching is beyond all reproach, that he is of distinguished origin and enjoys an equally distinguished reputation." Then he set out from Vicenza with Favre and Laynez for the last lap of his pilgrimage.

What Inigo had striven for since the luminous darkness by the Cardoner and through his efforts of many years seemed now well nigh fulfilment. He had united a small group of true followers under the standard of his crucified King. He is his own witness to the graces of this pilgrimage: "On this journey the pilgrim was visited by God in a most particular manner. Again and again he implored Our Lady to associate him with Her Divine Son."

At their last halt before Rome Inigo stepped into the tiny half-ruined chapel of La Storta. Once more he revealed to his Divine Master all that occupied his mind and heart. Then all of a sudden it was Manresa over again. A mystical illumination penetrated into the very depths of his being, an illumination which he would never again forget, and he felt impelled to describe it to his companions who were waiting by the roadside. Afterwards Laynez left a record of this significant hour. "As we were on the road from Sienna to Rome, it happened that our Father experienced many spiritual comfortings. He told me it was as if God the Father had impressed these words on his heart; 'I will be favourable to you in Rome.' Since our Father did not understand what these words would signify he added, 'I do not know what will happen to us, perhaps we shall be crucified in Rome.' Then he said it seemed to him as if he beheld Christ with the cross on His shoulder and by His side the Eternal Father who thus spoke to His Son: 'I desire You to take this man for Your servant.' Jesus accepted him with the words, 'It is my will that you serve Us.' Consequently he had an immense devotion to the name of Jesus and desired his company to be named 'The Society of Jesus'."

This vision of La Storta was for Inigo a seal from heaven upon the decisions taken at Vivarola, the supreme fulfilment of the prayer which he had taught them to utter in the crucial moments of the *Spiritual Exercises*: "to be enlisted under the standard of Christ in His poverty and ignominy." Years afterwards he recorded this vision in his mystical notebook. He held fast to the name by which his Society had been christened with the strength of a man whose knowledge has been deepened through mystical experience. This vision of their founder has always been recognised by his followers as one of the decisive moments of spiritual grace in his life. For it revealed in stark clarity the most profound nature of the Ignatian mysticism which is only hinted at in the *Spiritual Exercises*. The Eternal Father, Christ the God-man bearing the cross, the visible Church of Rome, the personal service of the man chosen by God's grace—all these are fused into a living unity. This is the heart-beat of the future Society of Jesus.

Father Nadal later interpreted this hour at La Storta for his brethren and added this appeal: "We must grow in a profound understanding of the thought that we are all followers of Jesus Christ who now as then carries His cross in the Church militant. Him we must follow with our own cross. For this purpose has the Eternal Father made us His servants."

It is here alone that can be found the "power and secret of the Jesuits". The painting over the High Altar in the Church of San Ignazio in Rome represents the vision at La Storta. Above it, in golden letters, runs this inscription: "I will be favourable to you in Rome."

I WILL BE FAVOURABLE TO YOU IN ROME
> Notes on the four plates that follow:

163 THE CATHEDRAL OF SIENNA
> A two weeks' journey on foot from Vicenza to Rome brought the pilgrims through Bologna, over the Apennine passes to Florence and Sienna.

164 AUTUMN JOURNEYING
> The northern shore of Lake Bracciano. From Sienna the three pilgrims walked along Lake Bolsena to Viterbo, thence the Via Cassia and the Via Claudia continue along both shores of Lake Bracciano as far as La Storta.

165 THE MYSTIC HALT
> The chapel at La Storta is three hours distant from the Eternal City. Even in ancient times it was the final resting-place before entering Rome. In its present form the chapel has been entirely renovated.

166 THE FINAL GOAL
> Inigo crossed the Tiber by the Milvian bridge in mid-November and entered the Eternal City through the Porta del Popolo. His pilgrimage was ended.

Inigo was indeed crucified in Rome in a sense far deeper than he had foreseen at La Storta. The Papal City was his Jerusalem which was to hold him prisoner till his death. Here at last Inigo became Ignatius, and his company of friends a religious order.

At first, the pilgrimage to Jerusalem that had bitten deeply into their consciousness remained in the foreground even at Rome. Lodging and activity they regarded as provisional. To begin with, the companions found shelter in the villa of the Patrician Quirino Garzonio on the slopes of the Pincio; later, at the beginning of June 1538, a house more favourably situated was rented for them by friends not far from the Ponte Sisto. Favre and Laynez began their lectures at the Sapienza, but with such poor success that Ignatius was ashamed. He himself was tireless in giving the *Spiritual Exercises*, to the influential Cardinal Contarini among others, and in the course of the work was on foot for hours each day. As the Lent of 1538 drew near, he went for forty days into the solitude of Monte Cassino with his now intimate friend Dr Ortiz. The Rome of these days had all too swiftly forgotten the horrors of the sack of the city. Luxury and hunger, sins and sanctity, were there side by side. But a genuine reform was taking shape; young Philip Neri was walking the city streets, Pope Paul III had issued shattering complaints in his document of reformation, Michelangelo was painting the *Last Judgment*. Ignatius said of the Rome of these days when he first met it: "I see all windows are shut." To his faithful friend, Señora Roser, in Barcelona, he wrote shortly afterwards: "Here the soil is poor in good fruit, and overgrown with bad."

The comrades waited in vain. War continued with the Turks. On February 8th, the League was renewed and war fleets sailed out of the harbour. There was now no hope of a pilgrim passage in this year during which they had been waiting. In consequence Ignatius summoned the companions from Northern Italy for fresh consultation in Rome.

But a new "war" flared up which was soon a matter of life and death for the little company. Agostino Mainardi, an Augustinian hermit and mighty orator, had preached the Lenten course in San Agostino. The "masters" from Paris scented beneath his flowery rhetoric the Lutheran heresy concerning Faith and good works. A friendly warning on their part only exasperated and antagonised the preacher, and his ardent disciples from the influential circle of Spaniards associated with the Curia. They retaliated with an attack on the company. Soon rumours were whispered throughout the city that the real heretics were these strange "reformed priests", who were fugitives from Spain and Paris and should be burned at the stake. The companions who on May 3rd had received canonical permission to preach, passed to the offensive, and from the Roman pulpits denounced the errors of the Augustinian. Ignatius wrote to Spain, that "this quarrel was taking up much of our time". The enemies' attack was directed in the main against Ignatius himself. Soon it was being said that the leader of these priests was named Inigo and was a man of evil reputation because of his scandalous behaviour. Pamplona was now re-enacted on a battlefield of the Lord. The Basque in Inigo prepared to give battle. He had started in Rome a suit against his calumniators which the Governor wanted to settle by a compromise. Ignatius would have none of it. He had testimonials to the teaching and life of his comrades sent from Ferrara, Bologna, and Sienna, and when these documentary weapons proved of no value, he left the city at the close of August and with grim determination went to Frascati where Paul III was then residing. During an hour's audience he told the Pope of his projects, of his experiences in prison at Alcalá and Salamanca, and insisted upon a solemn verdict—it was his first meeting face to face with the Vicar of the Lord who had promised him His favour in Rome.

On October 1st the companions moved from Ponte Sisto to a much roomier house that stood empty because it was supposed to be haunted. It was the property of a Patrician named Frangipani and lay near the Torre del Merangolo in what was then the fashionable quarter of the city. The little company dwelt there for two and a quarter years. It was here that Ignatius had the double experience of victory in the legal process and of the establishment of the Society of Jesus.

[76]

Then occurred what was, to use Ignatius's expression, "almost a miraculous business". The three men who had in the past made judicial enquiries into his orthodoxy chanced to be together in Rome at that moment, Figueroa from Alcalá, the Dominican, Ory, from Paris, and the Vicar-General de Dotti from Venice. Their testimony in his favour was conclusive. On November 18th Ignatius had in his hands the important document which attested that himself and his company, their teaching and the *Spiritual Exercises* were fully Catholic and beyond even the slightest suspicion of unorthodoxy. This conflict had lasted eight months. Meanwhile, in the international field of war the combined fleets of the League had suffered a disastrous defeat by the Turks on September 27th, but the end of the war was not in sight. Their year of delay was over. At one of the theological disputations which the companions held every fortnight in the Papal presence the Pope had remarked as if in jest: "Why are you so anxious to go to Jerusalem? Italy is a good and true Jerusalem for you if you desire to work fruitfully in the Church of God." Ignatius now grasped the vision of La Storta; he glimpsed again the light from the Cardoner in which he had once beheld the mystery of the Church as the Kingdom of God. All now pointed to one immense decision. With his little company he approached Pope Paul to place it and himself in fullest obedience at the Pope's disposition. The Pope was the head of the Church of Christ, his king, and that had been the substance of their vow at Montmartre. The date was between the 18th and the 23rd of November 1538. For the company of Jesus Rome took the place of Jerusalem: and this for ever. Alms collected for the pilgrimage were returned to benefactors. Ignatius wanted to begin a reform in Rome as the disciple of the King who had chosen poverty as his royal setting. It was with joy inexpressible that he celebrated his first Mass on Christmas Day in "Roman Bethlehem" at the altar of Christ's crib in Maria Maggiore.

In Rome the windows began to open. Ignatius knew full well how genuine reform within the Church must be inaugurated: not with programmes and solemn speeches but simply through an heroic effort of love where souls clamoured most insistently for alleviation. Throughout the winter of 1538–1539 the Eternal City suffered heart-breaking pangs of hunger. The dying lay in the streets, the starving children begged in doorways. Within a brief space the companions had housed hundreds of poor in the house of Frangipani and tended them with loving charity. A thrill of astonishment shook the city. Even Cardinals came by night to look at this unaccustomed devotedness. Ignatius had begun his work in Rome.

THE WINDOWS OPEN

Notes on the ten plates that follow:

167 THE SLOPES OF THE PINCIO

The villa in which Ignatius first found shelter stands in this garden but has been wholly rebuilt.

168 NEW ST PETER'S UNDER CONSTRUCTION

Behind the ancient Basilica with the wings that were added at a later period, may be seen the supports of the cupola then in process of construction. The picture shows the view Ignatius would have had of St Peter's and the Vatican.

169 THE ROMAN UNIVERSITY

The interior courtyard of the Sapienza was begun in the Pontificate of Leo X, according to plans laid down by Michelangelo; it was finished by della Porta in 1575. The upper storey was added later.

170 SPAIN'S PATRON SAINT

The statue of St. James, sculptured by Sansovina about 1520, stood in those days in the National Church of the Spaniards in the Piazza Navona. It was transferred to Santa Maria de Montserrato where Ignatius frequently preached.

171 SAN AGOSTINO

This travertine façade, begun in 1483 by Cardinal Estouteville, is one of the masterpieces of the Renaissance.

172–173 PAUL III, THE FARNESE POPE

The pontificate of Paul III (1534–1549) was a period bridging the Renaissance and Reform. Preoccupied with the prestige of his own family he initiated the construction of the massive Palazzo Farnese, but he also gave the Church the new religious order of Ignatius.

174 THE FIRST MEETING BETWEEN THE PONTIFF AND IGNATIUS

The former Papal palace in Frascati, built by Pius II, in which Ignatius visited the Holy Father.

175 THE OPEN HOUSE FOR THE POOR

Antonio Frangipani's house, on the left side of the street, was largely transformed in the second half of the sixteenth century.

176 THE GLORY OF GOLD OVER THE POOR CRIB

The coffer-work ceiling in Maria Maggiore was erected during the pontificate of Pope Callixtus III, whose family coat-of-arms (that of the Borgias) may be seen in the third series of inlaid bays. The royal consorts, Ferdinand and Isabella, presented the first gold brought from the New World for the decoration of this ceiling during the pontificate of Alexander VI. Under the magnificent triumphal arch with its fifth-century mosaics the crib of Christ is preserved and reverenced. In Inigo's day it stood in a side chapel which has since been reconstructed.

THE BIRTH OF THE SOCIETY OF JESUS

The Roman populace called these men, who soon became famous for their works of charity, the "pilgrim priests" or "reformed priests", and regarded them as religious of a novel type. One of the charges in the legal processes of previous months was that they had formed themselves into a religious order without ecclesiastical approbation. As a matter of fact, the companions had never contemplated such a step, not even at Vicenza. But now requests were reaching the Pope asking him to send some of these reformed priests to Mexico or the East Indies. Was this highest ideal of theirs, this obedience to the Pope to separate and scatter them throughout the world? Once again it was a decisive moment in the life of Ignatius. At the close of March 1539 the friends in the Frangipani palace started to clarify the issue with prayer and a sincere exchange of views. They were all agreed by April 15th and went to Communion together to celebrate the decision they had made: "We desire to remain permanently in an order and to take a vow of obedience to a superior whom we shall choose, in order to fulfil our vow to the Pope through regular channels and without imperilling humility." On May 3rd they set down their conclusions in eleven short paragraphs and by June 24th their minds were made up on all

 relevant points. The new order should have no special dress or penitential practices and would not sing the Divine Office: it should have houses of study for its young members and these might possess revenues; and it wished to be known as "the Society of Jesus". Towards the end of June Ignatius arranged these points together in the so-called "Summa Instituti", the first outline of the Constitutions of the Society. The document began with words intended to incorporate all his previous ideals: "Whoever will serve as a soldier in our society which we wish to be characterised by the name of Jesus, under God's standard of the cross, and to devote himself to our Lord alone and to his Vicar upon earth . . ."

Cardinal Contarini presented the document to the Pope, who had it carefully examined by the learned Dominican, Tommaso Badia, and was delighted to

be able to give an oral approval in the Papal palace at Tivoli on September 3rd. Enthusiastically, Ignatius sent off this news to Loyola: they must know at home what had happened to their preacher from Azpeitia. There now began a campaign at the Curia, lasting for a full year, against the revolutionary novelty of this plan for a new order. Cardinal Ghinucci in objection raised some fine points of Canon Law and made several emendations in the draft. Cardinal Guidiccioni brusquely rejected the idea of any new religious foundation and during the audience handled Ignatius quite severely. But Ignatius was once again the obstinate Basque whom nothing could dismay. He promised God three thousand masses, and bestirred himself. The King of Portugal, the Duke of Ferrara, and the cities in which the comrades had worked were all asked to send testimonials to Rome on their behalf. In May 1540 the atmosphere seemed favourable, only to be followed by a paralysing calm. Finally the end was reached through the good offices of Cardinal Carpi and after Guidiccioni had restricted the membership of the order to sixty. On September 27th 1540 the Bull "Regimini Militantis Ecclesiae" was promulgated in the palace of San Marco. The Society of Jesus had been established.

The Pope had given the companions the responsibility of working out constitutions for the new order. From March 4th 1541 onwards, this task was tackled by the "masters" of Paris who happened then to be at Rome. Naturally the most important question was the choice of a religious superior, the *Praepositus Generalis*. It was agreed that the superior should remain in office for life and his authority was defined. The election was held on April 2nd. Six of the friends from Paris took part in it: Ignatius, Laynez, Salmerón, Broét, Codure, and Jay. Favre was by this time in Germany, Xavier on the high seas on his way to India, Rodrigues in Portugal and Bobadilla in Calabria, but they had either left their votes recorded or despatched them to Rome. When the voting box was opened, it was seen that all of them had selected their master, Ignatius. On his own voting paper, without naming any particular person, Ignatius had written: "Myself excluded, I elect as superior the man who shall have the majority of votes." In profound alarm, he pleaded his state of health and the sins of his earlier life as reasons why he must decline the election. A new election on April 13th led to the same result. Ignatius withdrew for the three solemn days of Holy Week to the Franciscan Friary at San Pietro in Montorio. There he made full confession of the sins of his youth to Fra Teodosio, his confessor, and left the decision in his hands. This was given him in writing, to the effect that Ignatius must accept election, otherwise he would be sinning against the Spirit.

On Easter Tuesday the Society of Jesus had its first General. And now the happy day of Montmartre was lived over again. On the Friday of this decisive week, April 22nd 1541, the six religious walked at dawn out of the city to St Paul's beyond the walls. Ignatius celebrated Mass in what was then the chapel of the Blessed Sacrament with its old mosaic of Our Blessed Lady. Before the Communion he read aloud his vows of profession, written in his own hand, and afterwards the others read their formulas. They were united in the Divine Presence of their only Lord. We have Ignatius's description of the close of this unforgettable feast: "After Mass they met at the high altar, all five coming to Inigo and Inigo drawing near to them; he embraced each one singly and gave him the kiss of peace, amid deep affection and interior emotion, with tears of joy in his eyes. That is how they concluded the festival of profession which was the beginning of their apostolic calling. After it they experienced a profound and ever-growing peace, to the praise of our Lord Jesus Christ."

Little Pedro Ribadeneira, who a short time previously had run away from Cardinal Alessandro Farnese, in whose service he was a page, and had been accepted as a novice in the Frangipani palace, witnessed this festival. Indeed, not far from the church of the Lateran, to which pilgrims were streaming, he had prepared for them a brotherly meal. He never forgot this moment till his dying day. When the new Professed took their pilgrim way home from St Paul's, so wrote Ribadeneira, Master Jean Codure hurried ahead of them, steeped in joy: "we heard him cry out aloud to Heaven and God, so that he seemed almost bursting with happiness." Yes, it was just like that other happy day on Montmartre, where after their vows they sat until evening by the fountain of Saint Denis and delighted in their simple meal together. What then they dimly foreshadowed was now fulfilled. "They thanked God with tears that He had deigned in His courtesy to bring them so far, that He had allowed them, men from so many different nations, to grow together into one unity, and that He had given them the wonderful experience of this day." Ignatius himself remained tranquil in his happiness. "Gently and imperceptibly and like 'a wise fool'" (to employ the expression of one of his companions), God's grace had brought him from St Paul on the Cardoner to St Paul's beyond the Roman walls. He had been twenty years a pilgrim. Now he had reached his goal. The Society of Jesus had been established.

THE BIRTH OF THE SOCIETY OF JESUS

Notes on the six plates that follow:

177 GIVEN IN ROME AT ST MARK'S

So ends the document, in which Paul III approved the new Order on September 27th 1540. The Palazzo Venezia, his favourite residence, then bore this name, from the adjoining church of San Marco.

178 SAN PIETRO IN MONTORIO

Ignatius withdrew to this Friary before accepting the results of the election. In the courtyard, Bramante erected this so-called Tempietto in 1502, as a commission from the Catholic royal consorts of Spain.

179 VOTING PAPER WITHOUT NAME

In order to betray no preferences among his companions, Ignatius worked out this voting formula, declaring himself ready to cast a vote for a definite person if a majority decision had been reached.

180–181 THE VOW DAY IN ST PAUL'S BEYOND THE WALLS

Before this mosaic picture of Our Lady from the thirteenth century, Ignatius read the document containing his carefully drawn up vow formula. The five companions present put their life-promises in Ignatius's hands.

182 AFTER PROFESSION

The companions experienced that "profound and ever-growing peace", of which Ignatius speaks in the silence of the cloister at St Paul's.

[82]

Jhus

excluyendo ami mismo / doy mi voz /
enel señor nro para seer prelado aquel
q terna mas voz es para seerlo / he
dado mi determinate boni consulendo /
Si tame alacompania le parecera otra
asa / o Juzgare que es mejor / y amayor
gloria / de dios nro señor / yo soy
aparejado para señalar lo echa
en Roma . 5 . de abril , de 1541

Professio prelati

Ego subscriptus promitto oīpotenti deo et sūmo pōtifiri eius in terris vicario corā eius virgine matre et tota celesti curia, ac in presentia sorietatis perpetuā paupertatem, castitatem et obedientiam iuxta formā viuēdi in bulla sorietatis dūi ihu, et in eius cōstitutionibus derlaratis seu derlarandis cōtentam. Insup promitto sperialem obedientiam sūmo pontifici rirca missiones in bulla rontentas, Rursus promitt me ruratuzū vt pueri erudiantur in rudimētis fidei iuxta eandem bullam . . . . ones. Actum . . . . . . venetis . . . . . aprilis . 1541 in edibus sancti pauli extra muros

Ignatius
de loyola

Professio sulditox

Ego subscriptus promitto oīpotenti deo corā eius Regine matre et tota celesti ruria ar in presentia sorietatis, et tibi reuerende pater loru dei tenēti perre tuam paupertatem. castitatem et obedientiam, iuxta formā viuēdi in bulla sorietatis dūi ihu et in eius rostitutionibus derlaratis seu derla, randis rontentam, Insup promitto sperialem obedientiā sūmo pōtifiri rirra missiones in bulla rontentas, Rursus promitto me obediturū rirra eruditionem puerox in rudimentis fidei iuxta eandem bullā et rostitutioēs Actum Rome die venexis 22 die aprilis . 1541 in edibus sancti pauli extra muros

Claudius
Jaius

Pasrhasius broet

Jacobus loyyrrez

Johannes
Coduri

alphonsus
salmeron

THE SMALL BEGINNINGS OF GREAT WORKS

Now commenced the Roman years of work of the new General. From February 1541 the gradually increasing religious family dwelt in a tumbledown house near the little church of Santa Maria degli Astalli. It was so miserable that Salmerón once jokingly said you had to be predestined by grace to go on living in it. But the little church contained Ignatius's favourite picture of Our Lady of the Wayside. In September 1544 the Fathers were able to construct by the church a modest new house, in which the General had three small rooms. This was the "Professed House", from which Ignatius directed the Society until his death. Such was in fact the law of all the works, which Ignatius undertook for Rome and soon for the whole world: their beginnings were small, often miserably poor, and not infrequently an occasion of opposition. But they were so well planned and held to with such tenacity that a Cardinal once said: "When Ignatius drives home a nail, nobody can pull it out." Ignatius tackled just those problems, that souls were calling for. His original plans for Jerusalem were brought to realization in Rome. He soon had a house at the foot of the Capitol for Jews and Moors who wanted to become Catholics. In order to check moral decline in the city he founded the house of St Martha for prostitutes, and its first funds came from the sale of antique sculpture discovered during the building of the Professed House. The Renaissance was over. Ignatius collected distinguished men and women into a committee to look after the convent of St Martha and to assist him not merely in keeping the poor women as hitherto inside a convent, but in preparing them for a proper married life in the world. In 1547 the house contained more than a hundred women. Ignatius bothered his head very little about the consternation occasioned by this in Rome. One complaint to the Pope included the statement that "these priests want to reform the entire world". Ignatius went even further. His plan was to keep young people out of sin and he petitioned the Pope for leave to establish a home for girls whose morals were in danger, which he very soon set up near the church of Santa Catarina dei Funari. The orphanage of Santa Maria in Aquiro was continually assisted by him. His desire to see that the dying were spiritually cared for by genuinely Christian doctors led him to draw up a lengthy moral-theological memorandum for the Cardinals. Wherever there was new activity in Rome, you found Ignatius.

He was a tireless preacher during these years. Speaking in what was still an extraordinary mixture of Spanish and Italian, he was in the habit—so one listener declared—of ending nearly every sermon with these words: "to love God with all our hearts, with all our mind, with all our strength"—words that pierced like a sword through the listeners' souls. He taught catechism for young and old in the squares near the Pantheon, the flower market and the bankers' quarters. "And he never gave up speaking, even when the street arabs threw apples at him." People laughed at "these theatines, these queer birds" and one fine gentleman called the priests from the Astalli church "the dregs and refuse of the city of Rome". That was all right for Ignatius. That was how God's works began.

The General's plans were becoming more ambitious, even though, as his secretary remarked of these years, "he suffered often so severely from stomach pains that he could make no movement and lay simply helpless. He always felt better when some important matter had to be tackled, then he started to labour day and night." On one occasion Ignatius revealed the secret of his power of work: "To do the things of this world carelessly, that matters little: but it is quite unbearable that a man should not pay full attention to the things of God." He may have smiled in recollection of his Latin school bench at Barcelona as, in 1551, he was laying the foundation of the famous Roman College. But here too the beginning was poor and modest. He rented a small house at the Mercatello near the foot of the Capitol, and to its door was fastened a notice that would become immortal in the history of the reform of Church studies: "School of Grammar, Humanities and Christian Doctrine. Free." Soon no more scholars could be accommodated; the work was transferred to a new building near San Stefano del Cacco by the Piè di Marmo, which became the focal point of the Roman activity of Ignatius. One year subsequently, in October 1552, his consuming zeal started another work, which still continues: the college for German theologians. This also was initiated first in an old house near the Capitol, then by the Piè di Marmo; it also had the same setting of poverty and unbounded confidence in God. One day, when the wealthy Cardinals were no longer willing to provide the money promised for this work, Ignatius laconically remarked: "Very well, I shall keep the house going on my own, even if I have to sell myself."

That was Ignatius in his Roman years. But all his plans and creations were in a sense a side activity. His essential task was to draw up constitutions for his religious order and to direct the religious family now growing with amazing swiftness, from the Indies to Brazil, from Africa as far as Ireland. The Pope made increasing calls upon his wise counsel. Cardinals summoned him to their palaces. Ignatius was hours afoot even at night. He must frequently have spoken with Cardinal Mendoza of his prison-chains in Salamanca, when the eloquent Melchior Cano launched his fierce campaign against the new Order. We can sense the smile of Ignatius when his secretary wrote once to Salamanca: "You know—if I may speak in jest—those adversaries will never be on the same footing as Ignatius till each of them has had a chain on his leg." Ignatius journeyed in the Pope's service once to Montefiascone, and then at the request of the Farnese family to Tivoli and Castel Madama to re-establish peace between the two cities, as he had done in Guipúzcoa. Throughout two November weeks in 1552 he tramped in teeming rain to Alvito, in the Kingdom of Naples, to compose the marriage quarrel of the duchess Colonna. When his secretary tried to dissuade him from undertaking the journey Ignatius answered: "For thirty years now I have never let wind or rain or other difficulties keep me from starting punctually any work planned in the service of God our Lord."

While Ignatius laboured and suffered in his narrow room at Rome, the works of his brethren throughout the world flourished mightily. He would gladly have worked with them, his desire would have been to "walk barefoot to Portugal" or to pass his remaining days with the Berbers in Africa. But he remained fastened to the cross of his Roman exertions. This is how he could write to his spiritual child, Margareta, Duchess of Parma: "God our Lord marches on here in Rome and in every corner of the world, and for this He makes use of this least Society to the glory of His Divine Majesty."

THE SMALL BEGINNINGS OF GREAT WORKS

Notes on the six plates that follow:

183 THE FIGHT AGAINST POVERTY AND SIN

The home for girls in moral danger stood near the Church of Santa Catarina dei Funari, the building of which started under Cardinal Cesi in 1544.

184 THE FIRST JESUIT SCHOOL

Nothing is left of the pattern of streets and houses at the foot of the Capitol where the Roman College, later to become so famous, had its modest beginning. Today their place is taken by the handsome piazza in front of the Ara Coeli.

185 CONCERN FOR GERMANY

The second home of the German College was not far from the Piè di Marmo, the remains of a colossal antique statue from the ancient city in Rome.

186–187 IN TIVOLI

It was in the Rocca, constructed by Pius II, that Paul III in 1539 gave an oral approval to the Society. In 1549 Ignatius was present at the foundation feast of a college built in the vineyards of the former villa of Maecenas. He would have ridden along the old road from Rome through the city entrance, the Porta del Colle, into Tivoli itself.

188 IN THE HOUSE OF AN OLD FRIEND

The old interior court of what today is the Palazzo Pio. Then it was the residence of Cardina Mendoza.

188

THE FATHER'S LEGACY

From the day of his election Ignatius's most important task was to compose a constitution for his company. The spirit and power of his Society lay deeply concealed in the book of the *Spiritual Exercises*. These had brought him his first companions, and all those now streaming to join the company had to pass through their school. The text of the little book was basically fixed after the experiences at Paris and Manresa, but in his Roman years this sharpest of self-critics continued to perfect the work. In 1546 he had it translated into a fine Latin version and at the request of Francis, Duke of Borgia, he submitted this text to the Pope. On July 31st 1548 Paul III gave his blessing to this book which has transformed the world. That same year the *Spiritual Exercises* were published. On one occasion Ignatius spoke of them as follows: "They are the best that I could ever feel, think and understand in this life, with the object of helping many men in their struggle for perfection."

But this spirit required also a structural framework, the "interior law of love" needed an expression in formal terms. That was one of the fundamental experiences of this enthusiastic and withal prudent man. In 1541 Ignatius commenced to outline with his brethren the first sketches of a constitution. Everything was subjected to his slow and careful scrutiny. On March 14th 1544 the Pope had removed the limiting clause on membership of the Society and on June 5th 1546 he approved a novel idea of Ignatius, by which in addition to the Professed it might accept also priests and lay-brothers as so-called Coadjutors. That same year the General was forced to put up with some distressing scenes occasioned by his former benefactress, Isabel Roser. She had travelled to Rome with two other ladies to place herself under the authority of Ignatius. The ladies were received but they proceeded to create more trouble for the General than the direction of the entire order. After a tearful exhibition of reluctance to go, Ignatius had to dismiss them in peace. Shortly afterwards, the Pope laid down a permanent prohibition of any feminine branch of the new order. In the meantime, the number of members, especially of young students, was increasing rapidly. In consequence there arose the question, fundamental in the development of all religious orders, of the relation between absolute poverty and training in studies. From 1544 onwards, the former pilgrim of heroic poverty was struggling with this problem. His approach to it is given in his own words: "This was his method in drawing up the Constitutions; every day he celebrated Mass and there commended to God's attention the very point with which he was concerned. He then reflected upon it in meditation. Tears were the regular accompaniment of his prayers and Masses." A portion of his mystical diary for this year is preserved, and permits us a glance into the graces of this lofty soul. We see him struggling for clarity in the framing of the constitution: in the streaming tears that he notes calmly in its pages, in his vision of the Blessed Trinity, in the childlike prayer to Mary, his advocate, whose ancient and venerated picture in the neighbouring church was so dear to his heart. By the close of 1546 the first portion of the work had been formulated, the *Examen Generale*, which includes the most important questions and which the Society brings to the notice of every postulant. This was followed by the careful composition of the ten sections of the Constitutions themselves. To assist him Ignatius had a large number of preliminary sketches and records of discussion. But it was not until 1547 that the task of shaping this magnificently conceived structure could make real progress. From the beginning of this year he had an ideal collaborator in Father Juan de Polanco. With his finely trained theological mind and lucid legal temperament, he was the born secretary. He prepared rough drafts, copied extracts from the rules of Orders from Benedict to Dominic, understood how to adapt himself with sensitive modesty to his master, to whom he was entirely devoted, and saw that Ignatius had time for writing undisturbed. Frequently Ignatius went to a friend's quiet garden to work in peace. In October 1547 Polanco wrote to Spain: "One responsibility has cost our Father a great deal of time. It is his work on the Constitutions, which with God's grace will keep our Society in good estate and greatly advance it. It is necessary work, but it demands a large amount of time and is laborious."

At the conclusion of 1549 the work was, in the main, finished. In the Jubilee year of 1550, when the foundation members of the Society were summoned to Rome, the General circulated the text for their considered opinions. The text was discussed in brotherly charity, and then unanimously approved. Even this did not satisfy Ignatius with his rare knowledge of men. He took years to test the Constitutions, gathering new impressions—in which the tireless Father Nadal was of valuable assistance in his journeys throughout Europe—and he added them to the text to improve it. Only death could take the pen from his hand. But then the Constitutions of Ignatius were complete for all time. This nail too had now been driven home—a turning-point in the Church's law on religious orders had been reached.

When Pope Julius III gave a new and solemn approval to the Society of Jesus on July 21st 1550, Ignatius could offer undying gratitude to God for the work which His grace had allowed him to complete. The Eternal Father had been gracious to him in Rome, the revelations along the Cardoner had become reality. For some of the smallest points of the Constitutions he had gone back to the light vouchsafed him at Manresa. Since those graces given to him then, in his "wise unwisdom", he had been led along the pathway of divine dispensation to his goal. His life's task appeared fulfilled. Father Nadal heard him repeat frequently: "I have asked God to grant me three graces before I die, in the first place the confirmation of the Society of Jesus by the Holy See, secondly a similar approval of the *Spiritual Exercises*, and thirdly that I might be able to write down the Constitutions." Years afterwards the same Father Nadal gave a spiritual exhortation to his brethren in Alcalá, where Inigo was once held prisoner: "Our Father Ignatius was a man of lofty character, with a spirit that was all-embracing. With these natural gifts and the grace of our Lord, he put all his energy into great enterprises. All his activity was shot through with a flame of zeal. Look at his Society, his Institute, his *Spiritual Exercises*: they are all a living source of love and ardour, a keenness that can never slacken, an abiding appeal and impulse to a generous help for souls. Don't you realise that we are at war, that we are on the field of battle? God's soldier must be no idle warrior."

This was the Ignatian spirit which inspired the first Jesuits.

THE FATHER'S LEGACY

Notes on the six plates that follow:

189 THE BOOK THAT CHANGED THE WORLD

Ignatius continued to improve the text of his *Spiritual Exercises* until 1548, the year when it was printed. The margin of this page, containing the meditation on the birth of our Lord includes two additions in his handwriting about the cave at Bethlehem which were incorporated in the final text.

190 OUR LADY OF THE WAYSIDE

This deeply devotional fourteenth-century picture of Mary was transferred from the church of the Astalli to a chapel in the newly constructed church of the Gesù and in later times richly ornamented.

191 FROM THE SPIRITUAL DIARY

This page comprises the days from April 29th to May 11th 1544 which with the previous thirty-three days were devoted to considering what principles were to be employed in selecting the work for the Society. Each day Ignatius noted whether he had the gift of tears or not ("con lagrimas" or "sin ellas"), and to see with a glance he inserted the capital letter "L" before each mention of the gift. On Sunday, May 11th, he refers to "the inward speech" and "the heavenly harmony".

192-193 THE RULE BOOK OF THE SOCIETY

Ignatius included in the "Principles Old and New" (Determinaciones antiguas y nuevas) the results of years of preliminary work and discussion. The text of the Constitutions that was laid before the companions in 1550, he continued to work on as General with his own hand until his death. Here is an example from the fourth chapter of the *Examen Generale* referring to the obedience to be shown even when working in the kitchen under the cook.

194 GRATITUDE TO THE POPE

A seventeenth-century painting that hangs in the Sacristy of the Gesù. It is "in memory of Pope Paul III", a memory treasured in the Society which he approved and confirmed.

(left column, partially visible)
nasciendo y otros muriendo...
mas diuinas, como en ell su soli...
uestad como miran toda la...
las las gentes en tanta ce...
mendose al infierno. ȝ vera...
...y...for sacar.

...sar sobre la haz dla tier...
...con otros, como juran y
...den las personas diuinas
...del genero humano ꝗ
...el fin ȝ: y reflotir despues
...palabras:

...las personas sobre la haz dla
...ni...mis... assi mismo ꝉ
...sabor obrando la santissima
...lo ꝗ hazen el angel y nuestra...
...ziendo su officio delegado
...y haziendo gracias ala di...
...officio para sacar algun...

...cio, pensando lo que deuo...
...cutan o al verbo eterno en...
...noça nuestra, pidiendo se...
                                ꝯ

(main right page)

qensi sentiere para mas seguir ꝯ y imitar al señor nuestro, ansi
nueua mente ~~imsecto~~ encarnado deziendo vn pr̃ mr̃.

La Segunda cõtemplaciõ es del nascimiento

<table>
<tr><td>orõ</td><td>La solita oraciõ p̃paratoria.</td></tr>
<tr><td>1 p̃ambulo</td><td>El primer preambulo es la hystoria, y sera aqui, como desde
nazaret salieron nuestra señora grauida, quasi de nueue me
ses asentada en vna asna y Josep y vna ancila llenando</td></tr>
<tr><td>Como se
puede me
dotar piã
mente</td><td>vn buey para yr a bethelem, a pagar el tributo ꝗ Cesar
hecho en todas aquellas tierras fol. 41. ḟ. a b.</td></tr>
<tr><td>z. p̃.</td><td>El segundo cõposicion viendo el lugar sera aqui. con la
vista ymaginatiua ver el camino desde Nazaret a beth
lem. considerando la longura la anchura. y si llano. o
si por valles o cuestas sea el tal camino. asi mismo mi</td></tr>
<tr><td>F el lugar
ó ospe lun
ca del naci
miento</td><td>rando el lugar ~~del ~~ quan grande quan pequeño
quan baxo, quam alto, y como estaba aparejado.</td></tr>
<tr><td>3 p̃.</td><td>El 3 sera el mismo y por la misma forma ꝗ fue en la
precedente cõtemplacion.</td></tr>
<tr><td>1 puncto</td><td>El primer puncto es ver las personas, es a saber ver a mi
señora y a Joseph y a la Ancilla, y al niño Jesu, despues
de ser nascido haziendo me yo vn pobrezito y esclauito
indigno mirandolos, cõtemplandolos, y siruiendolos, en</td></tr>
</table>

34 L martes conlaprimas

35 L mjercoles ~~asimesmo~~ conlaprimas

36 L Juebes asi mjesmo conlaprimas

37 Viernes sjnellas

38 L Sabado conellas

39 L domingo conellas

40 L lunes ⎤
41 L martes ⎦ mepareçe conellas

42 mjercoles ⎤
43 Juebes ⎦ meparece sjnellas
44 martes

45 L sabado comuchas enella

46 a. L domyngo antes delamjsa conlaprimas yenella o muy
abundamas dellas yco tjmados, yio loqnela dela mjsa
~~io pareçere mas tjmjntes dada~~ y abiendo demandado el
mjsmo dia por toda la semana qnto hallaua halo
qnela exteena quto no hallaua y la mteena menos, avn
y el sabado paçado hallaua vn poco mas apreado /aspmjs
mo en todas las mjsas delasemana a my no tan aspten
dos delaprimas io mas contenta mj enlamjsa por el gusto dela
loytas o denoa y otras algunas veçes q
enparte del temalaprimas / las de este dia me pareçia mu
cho mjs diuersas de todas otras pasadas por vem
tanto tencas mternas smaues sjnestecpo como hono creaedla ypaee
y vemja tanto detento sjnsabei explicar / yenla loylj mteena vex teena

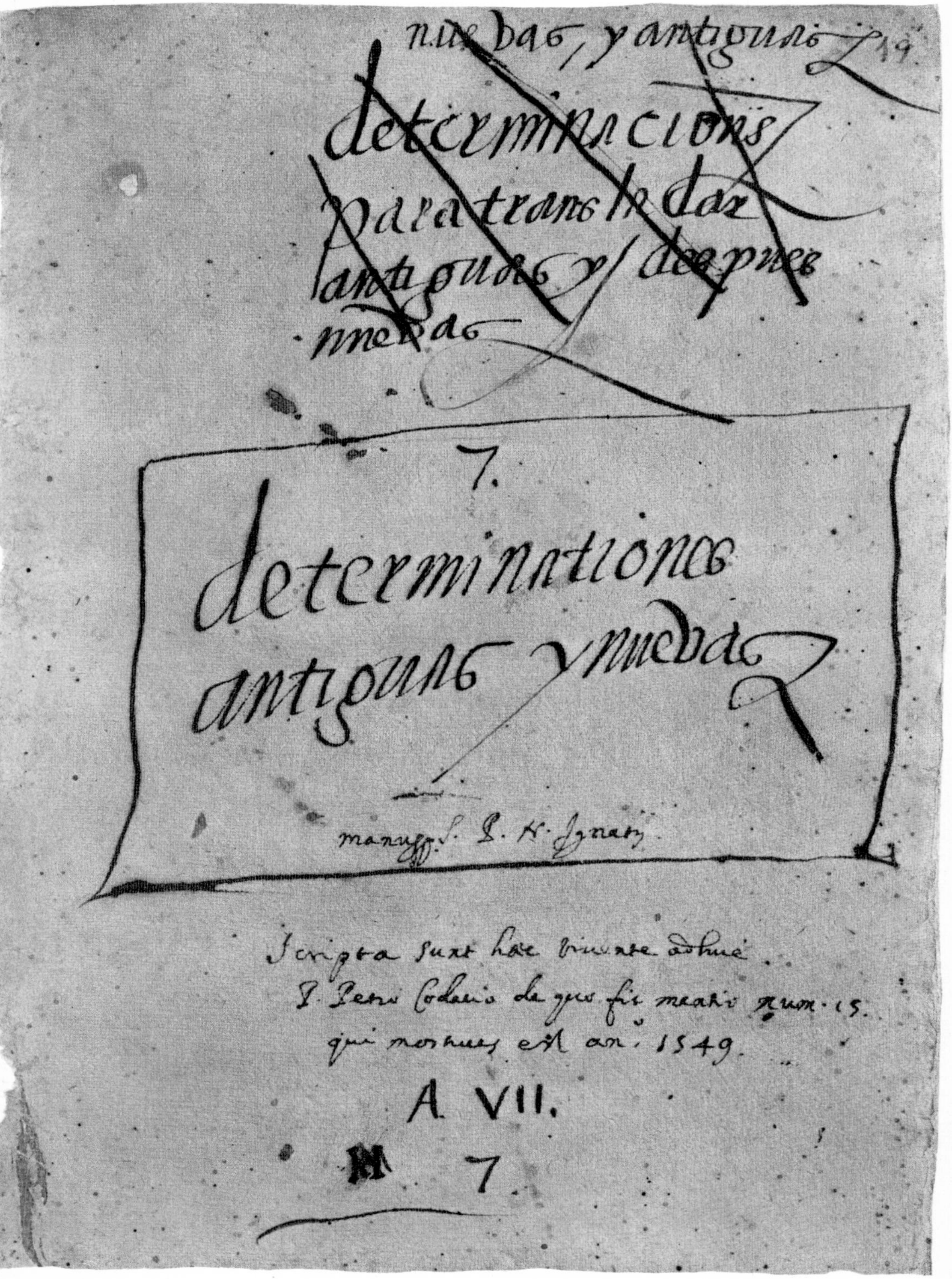

nuevas, y antiguas 19

determinacions

para transladar

antiguas y/ de espues

nuevas

7.

determinationes

antiguas y nuevas

manusc. S. P. N. Ignatij

Scripta sunt haec vivente adhuc

P. Petro Codacio de quo fit mentio num. 15.

qui mortuus est an. 1549.

A VII.

M 7

hazed esto, o aquello por que si le ruega parecera mas
que habla como hombre a hombre, y vn secular
cozinero, rogar avn sacerdote q limpie las ollas
o haga otras cosas similes no parece que es ho-
nesto ni justo, mas mandandole o diziendole
que haga esto o aquello ~~parece q~~ mostrarla mas habla
como christo a hombre, pues en su lugar
le manda y asi la persona que obedeçe
deue considerar y ponderar la voz q del
cozinero, o de otro q le sea superior sale, como si
de christo Nro Sor saliese, para ser entera
mente agradable a la su diuina Magad

Esto mismo se entienda en los otros officios
baxos quando alguno ayudare en ellos
y de la misma manera se tome en los
officiales subordenados que con tanto aucto-
ridad del superior gouiernan la Casa / 8 leela

En el tiempo delas enfermedades no solo
deue obseruar la obediencia con mucha
puridad alos superiores spñales para que
gouiernen su anima mas avn cõ la misma
summidad alos medicos corporales y enfermeros

194

THE NARROW ROOM AND THE WIDE WORLD

At the close of 1550 the General of the Order lay sick to death in his poor bedroom. What his soul experienced in those days he was later to reveal: "In his judgment and in the verdict of others this was his death sickness. The thought of death brought him so much joy, the inner comfort that death was nigh was so overwhelming, that he dissolved into tears. This grew to be so regular a happening that he refused to think of death to avoid the excess of consolation."

On January 30th 1551 Ignatius placed before the assembled brethren a letter, "on which he had reflected for months and years". It contained in seven weighty sentences his resolve to lay down the office of General. The brethren were alarmed by the sixth of these sentences which ran thus: "Thinking earnestly on all these things I lay down my office in the name of the Father and the Son and the Holy Ghost, my one God and Creator, and I resign absolutely and irrevocably the power that I have in it. I beg and implore with my whole soul that this my request will be accepted since it is justified in the sight of His Divine Majesty."

The sons refused to accede to the Father's request. Without a word Ignatius accepted their decision. The very next day a bundle of important letters was again despatched. And now we have this astonishing development. From this time to his death the General's field of work grew wider until it was beyond all measurement. His low room with the heavy roof joists seemed to burst asunder with the wealth of idea and counsel that went out from it to every part of the world where his Society was active. "Rome is the heart of the Society", wrote the indefatigable secretary, Polanco, "because the members of the Society have their origin there and because it is from Rome that a living force streams out to them all." We possess 920 letters from Ignatius up to the close of the year 1549; to the time of his death there follow no less than 6,641 either personally written or entrusted to his secretary. These statistics are sufficient evidence of the thorough greatness of this man who had lost all sense of self. Ignatius composed long circular letters on obedience, on the care of humanistic studies, on true and false mysticism, and even on a naval plan to counter the threat from the Turks. He corresponded with princes and high-born ladies, with simple folk and generous benefactors; he comforted dis-heartened brethren, and when need arose maintained discipline in his Order with the sharpest censure. His secretary he handled ruthlessly until letters were neatly finished and exactly copied. The seal, with which he added the signature of Jesus to his documents, had become the weapon of this warrior of God. Side by side with these were the day-to-day worries about the enlargement of Church and residence, now far too small, and his numberless visits to the palace of the Papal Chancellery. He concerned himself with pious requests for relics from Queen Catherine of Portugal, once the lady of his heart at Torde-sillas, with legal processes brought by the Duchess of Parma, with the case of the aunt of Cardinal Mendoza attracted by Luther's heresy—they all came to him, this wise counsellor and helper in a thousand needs. Nothing availed to ruffle his Basque serenity, not the financial straits of the residence, nor the legal wrangling of neighbours, not even the peacock's cries in the garden nearby. His immensely wide spirit spanned the world, even for the modest necessities of day to day.

This small and ageing man—he was scarcely five feet three in height—walked through the Roman streets in cassock and wide-brimmed felt hat, concealing beneath the simple dignity of refined character a richly affectionate heart. The source of his strength was his individual prayer, and for hours on end during the night he might pace his room in meditation. He said Mass in his study before a painting of the Holy Family, but in his last years, sickness and, at the same time, his mystical consolations, rarely permitted him to celebrate Mass. His soul was open wide to the Divine Presence, he could discover his Triune Creator as he looked up at the shining stars, in flowers or in the whirl of Roman streets. By comparison, as he admitted, the graces received at Man-resa were only a gentle introduction. At times, while hearing the liturgy sung in church, "he found himself swept swept high aloft"—this was his confession to one of his brethren—"and this not only benefited his soul, it helped him to recover his bodily health. And so, when he was ill or depressed, nothing comforted him as effectively as a pious hymn sung by a fellow Jesuit." Philip Neri, his joyous friend, frequently observed a strange light flit across the face of Ignatius. No one could withstand the penetrative look in his eyes. One member of his community noted that "he knew you at once from head to foot". When his friends attempted to seize on the essential quality of this remarkable man, no expression was more often used than "magnanimous". Ignatius is the man with an immense heart. Difficult to describe him except in contradictions. He was impetuous and yet highly prudent, stern but also joyful; "grace in him had become second nature". Outwardly laconic and reserved, he once commented: "Were a man to measure my love by its outward expression, he would be very wide of the mark." To the most outstanding of his brethren like Laynez and Polanco "he gave hard bread to digest". Yet his community often remarked that "any man coming from his room always looked cheerful". "The little Spaniard who limped a bit and had such laughing eyes"—that is how Ignatius was spoken of in these years.

One of his brethren testified that during the final days of his life Ignatius was concerned almost exclusively with the development of the Society. Its growth was phenomenally rapid and might well cause him anxiety. As early as 1549 he had said to Ribadeneira: "Pedro, another ten years and we shall see great things: I shan't see them myself but you will." And so it happened. At the death of its founder the Society had twenty houses in Italy and nineteen elsewhere. In 1550 it was divided into three administrative regions, Portugal, Spain, and the Indies, known as provinces. By 1556 ten further provinces had been created for about 1,000 members. Of this number, in addition to the surviving first companions, only thirty-eight were Professed Fathers, such was Ignatius's insistence on the way of poverty and the cross. As the Father lay on his death-bed in the same room from the window of which he had so often looked upon the stars, Polanco, so loyal to his memory, recorded in his chronicle of the Order, thinking of the realms that had been won for Christ: "And so he who fifteen years before had established the Society and had directed it since its foundation was privileged by God's grace to see it established in so many places."

THE NARROW ROOM AND THE WIDE WORLD

Notes on the eight plates that follow:

195 THE HOLY FAMILY

Ignatius used to celebrate Mass in his study before this picture by an unknown painter of the fifteenth century.

196–197 THE NARROW ROOMS

Ignatius directed his Order from these "camarette", which are all that today remain of the old Professed House. The open doorway leads to the small balcony with a view on to the garden.

198 THE GENERAL'S SEAL

The first three letters of the Holy Name "I. H. S.", have, since Ignatius's time, been the seal and emblem of the Society of Jesus.

199 THE GENERAL AND HIS SECRETARY

Polanco wrote this letter to Rodrigues in Lisbon on July 2nd 1550 "on behalf of our Father in Christ, Master Ignatius". The General corrected the draft and added a postscript in his own handwriting.

200 THE PAPAL CHANCELLERY

The Palace of the Cancelleria, begun in 1489, was the centre of ecclesiastical administration. Its spendid inner courtyard was built to plans of Bramante.

201 THE WEARINESS OF OFFICE

The second page of the document in which Ignatius announced and gave explicit reasons for his resignation of office. As was the case at his election ten years previously, he began by pointing to his sins and sickness. In the involved and solemn manner that was characteristic of the man, the seventh sentence reads as follows: "Should there be any difference of opinion among those whose task it will be to take this declaration and adjudge it to the greater glory of God, I beg them for the most reverent love of God our Lord, that they would recommend this question to His Divine Majesty, that in all things His most Holy Will be done to His greater glory, to the greater and general good of souls and of the whole Society. May they accept it all for God's higher praise and for His honour for ever."

202 OUR LADY ABOVE THE WRITING TABLE

In his account of his work on the Constitutions Ignatius himself declared: "At times he beheld the Blessed Virgin as she interceded with God or gave her own approbation." Father General Oliva assures us that this picture, the work of an unknown artist of the Umbrian school, hung in Ignatius's study. It is now in Genoa.

y el nos cōſerue y adelante en ſu ſ[anto] ſerui[cio] continuamēte
[co]del jubileo impetrado de todos los q eſtan alla en portugal y
en las Indias, y dōde qu[i]era ſe obediēcia dela cōmiſſo ya ſe ſcri
uio por otras, viſitādo 4 yglesias (o una 4 vezes por 30 dias cōtinuos
(o interpolados/ no dire mas por eſta ſino q eſtamos deſeoſos
de ver a v. R. ſi ſera ſeruido dios n. s. y ſu fl. y entonzes q nos
alargaremos en muchas cōſas cō ſuauidad y fauor el qual nos de
ho ſeruirle cōtinuamēte y ſu mag. de Roma 2 de Julio. 1550

de   2.   R.   ſieruo en x[rist]o

Comiſsion de n[uest]ro en x[rist]o ſe[ñor] m[i] ignatio   Joan de polanco

en eſta miſ ma petiçion dio pues dela cōceſſio del
Jubileo y otras pias ſpiritu[ales] / cerca renouerar las
temporal es q̄ demadri impugna cō ſu n[uest]ro p. ſu
ſādad deziendo q queria hazer una limoſna
al n[uest]ra caſa, d[ij]o cargo al uno delos aſsistentes que
le ayudaſe, teniēdo a dezir q el queria ha
zer la tal limoſna, mas adelāte ſe dize en p[rincipi]o
y le mando dos bezes por [e]ſ... in virtud de obedi
encia q̄ todas las vezes que tubieſe neceſsidad
le bas y a alhablar y aga lizenzia a ſu ſādad
eſto / ſeos eſcribe no por loy. Con alimoſna
mas por q vea iō y dexō otros adiuō n[uest]ro ſ[eño]r
a eſta nueua cōpañia / tanto amor y boluntad, cerca
eſta miſma cōpañia /

4 y eligiendo a la tal persona, deseo a si mismo que al tal se diese el tal cargo /

5 y no solamente me acompaña mi deseo, mas juzgando lo con mucha razon, para que se diese el tal cargo, no solo al que hiziere mejor y no tan mal, mas al que hiziere ygnalmente

6 esto todo considerando en el nonbre del padre, del hijo y del spu sancto un solo mi dios y mi criador, yo depongo y annuncio simplemente y asolutamente el tal cargo que yo tengo / demandando y en el señor mio con toda mi anima llorando de a los professos como a los y mas ynertes para ello / quieran aceptar esta my oblaçion assi justificada en la su diuina magestad

7 y si entre los que esto han de admitir y juzgar a maior gloria diuina se hallasse alguna discrepancia por amor de dios nro sor demando lo quiera mucho encomendar a la su diuina magestad para que en todo se aga su sma volutad a maior gloria suya y maior bien uniuersal de las almas y de toda la compañia, tomado esto todo en su diuina y maior alabança y gloria para siempre, en Roma oy viernes 30 de henero de 1551

Ignatio

THE MEN WITH IGNATIUS

The work of Ignatius succeeded because among his thousand sons were men who had learnt from him "to distinguish themselves in the service of the Eternal Lord of all things", and who proved the truth of another of their master's sayings: "The man who could not get on in the world is not suitable for the Society." Their lives are a proof of the greatness and limits of that ideal in which Ignatius had trained them.

There at his desk in Rome sat the ever-faithful secretary, Juan de Polanco. "Nine full years was he the General's hand and foot and carried the Society on his shoulders", was Ribadeneira's tribute to him. His brethren used to remark: "Even if somebody were a Polanco, Ignatius would tower above him as a wise, experienced man over a child."

The Father's thoughts often turned back to the unforgettable days at Paris where he had won his "nine dear friends in our Lord", by means of the *Spiritual Exercises*. Their names stood next to his own in the acts of the Society's foundation, firm and clear like irrevocable oaths. First Jean Codure. Death was his sole destiny in the Society, for he died shortly after the vow day at St Paul's. Next stood the name of the Benjamin of the Paris companions, Alfonso Salmerón, whose perilous missions to Ireland and Poland brought nothing but joy to his Father. At one time the name of Claudius Jay became a storm centre. This intelligent and charming Frenchman proved so valuable to the Emperor Ferdinand in Vienna that in 1546 he wanted him promoted to the bishopric of Trieste. Ignatius went into action at once: his whole religious ideal was threatened by this offer of ecclesiastical dignities. By night he hastened from Montecitorio up to the Borgo to enlist the support of Cardinals to prevent it. It was a proverb at the time that "when there were unpleasant things to be done, then the Father became fit again all of a sudden". Jay died in 1552 in Vienna in the precious liberty of that poverty which he had vowed along with Inigo at St Paul's.

There were two names in the 1540 document which Ignatius could not read without tears, tears both of sadness and of joy. "Simon Roderici", this was how Rodrigues the ever-beloved friend, had signed his name. In 1540 he had gone to Lisbon and become the centre of the flourishing province of Portugal. Later, however, he was at serious cross purposes with Ignatius who on that occasion, in 1553, sent his famous Letter on Obedience to Portugal. With touching words he summoned the offender to Rome: it was one of the darkest hours of his life when he had to threaten him with dismissal. But in November 1553 the two friends met face to face and all was buried in love's oblivion. In Bassano Rodrigues found his way back to the ideals of Montmartre. From there he wrote to his Father in 1555, "It is just eighteen years since your Reverence came to me here as I lay on the bed of death. God then restored to me the life of my body, do you give me back by your prayers the life of my soul." Rodrigues was always his problem child as Bobadilla, obstinate, rough and ready, was the madcap he was always defending. They were no saints, but men who worked indefatigably for God. Ignatius had borne with them and fashioned them.

There was another name: Francis. The nobleman from the castle of Xavier in Navarre was his greatest son. In 1450 he had had that unforgettable talk with Francis when the appeal came from the far Indies. "Master Francis, that is indeed an enterprise for you." Francis replied: "Good, that's fixed, I will do it"; nothing further. He patched up his cassock and set out—for India and Japan, until his lonely death at the gates of China. From there he wrote on his knees "to his one and only Father in the love of the Heart of Christ". Much later one of his brethren spoke thus in his praise: "Francis could not contain within Europe the width of his mind and his fire of energy. With Jesus as leader and Ignatius as guide he crossed the ocean, conquered the icy cold of Japan and the torrid heat of India."

In 1540 Diego Laynez had been absent on one of his missions in Italy. He was the most gifted theologian of them all, tough as only a Castilian can be tough, warmly attached to his master Inigo. He represented the new order at the Council of Trent with great distinction. No one was more qualified to take over the burden of responsibility after the General's death. He died in 1565 in the same room as Ignatius. He had fought God's battles with his pen. Ignatius was proud of him.

Already in 1546 Peter Favre, the Savoyard, had died in Rome, Peter the first-born of Inigo's sons in Paris. He could interpret the *Spiritual Exercises* of his master more sensitively than all the rest; in a spirit of quiet detachment he journeyed tirelessly across Europe, from Portugal to Germany. He had brought to Ignatius two men of the greatest calibre: Peter Canisius, apostle of the North, and the Spanish Duke, Francis Borgia. News of the entry into the order of this grandee, Ignatius wrote, "had the effect of a cannon shot". To the new recruit whose admission was a real triumph for the Society, still suspect in certain quarters, he declared: "We feel encouraged to begin with fresh energies to serve our Heavenly Father, now that he has sent us such a brother." They met in the Jubilee Year of 1550 and it was the Duke's happiest consolation to live in the poor Professed House and wait at table. Borgia's spiritual formation cost Ignatius considerable effort and we are indebted to it for some of his finest letters on mysticism. Ignatius for Borgia was the master whom he revered and loved. "Favre was a giant," he wrote, "but by comparison with Ignatius he was a child." Borgia celebrated his first Mass on August 1st 1551 in the castle chapel at Loyola—on the very spot where once Ignatius, recovering his health, had thanked God for the graces of the new life in Christ. When Ignatius died, Borgia, his indefatigable representative in Spain, wrote with deep emotion: "Our good Father has gone home to joy and to the happy harvest which he sowed amid ceaseless tears." After the death of Laynez he shouldered the burden of Ignatius's office till his death in 1572. He too breathed his last in the room of Ignatius.

These were the men with Ignatius. The secret of their great achievements they had learned from him: "Once our heart has been transformed, small wonder if the world is transformed through us." When the Portuguese Ambassador in 1540 requested six of the companions for the Indies, Ignatius answered—and his light-hearted reply concealed the greatness of his spirit—"Good gracious, My Lord Ambassador, and whom would you leave me for the rest of the world?"

[97]

THE MEN WITH IGNATIUS

Notes on the six plates that follow:

203 SIX OF THE FIRST TEN

Ignatius, Jean Codure, Simon Rodorici (Rodrigues), Alphonsus Salmerón, Claudius Jaius (Jay), Franziscus (Xavier). On March 4th 1540 when this document was signed, Favre and Laynez were in Parma, Bobadilla at Naples, Broët in Sienna.

204–205 IGNATIUS'S GREATEST SON

The home of St Francis, from which he derived his name, the castle of Xavier in Basque Navarre.

The main building with the latticed window and the East wing with its Gothic door are from the thirteenth century. The family coat-of-arms was added by Xavier's father. After the Spanish conquest of Navarre in 1516 the fortifications were demolished and the ruined foundation of the drawbridge may still be noted. The Apostle of the Indies died in 1552 in the Far East. His right arm with which he wrote to his Father Ignatius and baptized thousands, was brought to Rome in 1615, and is venerated in the church of the Gesù opposite the altar of the tomb of Ignatius.

206 THE FAITHFUL SECRETARY

The family vault of the Polancos in the church of St Nicholas at Burgos, an indication of the wealth of this family of distinguished merchants, was constructed at the beginning of the sixteenth century by the artist Francis of Cologne. The same artist was responsible for the remarkable stone relief work on the high altar, a gift of the Polanco family whose vault is to the right of the altar. Juan de Polanco, born 1517, already enjoyed a profitable post in the Roman Curia when he entered the order in 1541 and "was trained by the master hand of Ignatius". From 1547 onwards he was the General's tireless co-operator.

207 THE SECOND GENERAL

Diego Laynez took over the provisional direction of the Society after Ignatius's death and in 1558 was elected General by the First General Congregation. This picture, which was preserved from the beginning of the seventeenth century in the former Curia of the Society, represents him as the great theologian. But by the side of his book lies the sealing stick of the founder of the Society.

208 DUKE AND SAINT

The death mask of St Francis Borgia, third General of the Society of Jesus, who died in 1572. It is now preserved at Loyola.

poterint determinare ac si tota societas
sic in placuit et bis my fuit o169 Igno
540.

Ignatius   Johannes codur

Simon rodorici   Alphonsus
                          salmeron

                          Franciscus

Claudius
Jaius

208

A VERY ORDINARY DEATH

The work that Ignatius had created on earth was great. But Christian greatness is first confirmed by death and in that hour Ignatius was, perhaps, at his greatest. He died, so wrote Polanco, "a death like that of any ordinary man". Already in June 1553 the General had once remarked that "under his doctors' hands" he felt very near death. A year later he was weary unto death but was able to dictate his autobiography. He suffered unspeakable pains from gallstones which exhausted his remaining strength. In July 1556 the death he had long desired at heart entered his dark room.

Early in this July Ignatius tried to relax for three weeks in the small villa near Santa Balbina. But in vain. Quietly he returned to the Professed House and awaited death as something about which no bother should be made. On Thursday July 30th he discussed current business at supper as had been his habit for many years. Then he requested the secretary to go as soon as possible to the Vatican to ask for a last blessing from the Pope. The doctor saw no immediate danger, and Polanco mentioned that he had a large post to finish that night. At once Ignatius gave way. "Do what you think best, I leave myself entirely in your hands": that was all, it was at the same time his last word to his Society. The lay brother in the adjoining room heard him quietly praying at midnight: "O my God." When they went in to see him in the grey of dawn on July 31st he lay at his last gasp. Polanco hastened at once to the Vatican, but when he returned with the blessing of Paul IV, Ignatius was already dead. Without the Last Sacraments he had departed quietly and without a word. Father de Freux, who once had cheered him up in hours of depression by playing the clavichord, was praying at his bedside. The Father's soul was now where in his mystical diary it had longed to be, there where the music of heaven is heard and the ineffable words of the Eternal God.

"He died," wrote Polanco, "without blessing us, without naming a successor, leaving the Constitution unconfirmed, without any of those significant gestures with which other servants of God have taken their earthly leave—a death like that of any ordinary man." On the evening of August 1st his body was interred in the church of our Lady of the Wayside. On the gravestone was this inscription: "For Ignatius Loyola, founder and first General of the Society of Jesus, this stone is set by the companions and sons fashioned by him in Christ, for their good and beloved Father."

A VERY ORDINARY DEATH

Notes on the eight plates that follow:

209 THE LAST SPELL OF REPOSE

The villa of the Roman College which shortly before Ignatius's death had been constructed at the cost of great effort lay on the slopes of the Aventine. From it the sick man's view ranged over the ruins of the Baths of Caracalla.

210 A PAPAL BLESSING THAT CAME TOO LATE

In the grey morning light of July 31st 1556, Polanco hurried through the old Zecca entrance of the Vatican to the Pope. At that same hour Ignatius died.

211 THE DEATH MASK

The wax mask, taken immediately after his death and later for some time in the possession of the Empress Maria Theresa, bears the marks of his very varied experience. Today it is preserved in the Curia of the Society in Rome.

212–213 AS ARTISTS SAW HIM

Jacopino del Conte, one of the saint's former penitents, tried to perpetuate the dead man's features on the day of his death. But his contemporaries were not wholly satisfied with the picture. In 1585, Ribadeneira commissioned Sánches Coello, Philip II's court painter in Madrid, to paint a further portrait, using a different death mask. On seeing this portrait a Cardinal who knew Ignatius intimately exclaimed: "Yes, there he is, that is just himself." The original was burnt in 1931 in the attacks on the Church in Spain. During his lifetime Ignatius had always refused to have his portrait painted.

214, 215–216 THE SAINT

This head, preserved in the Curia of the Society at Rome, was made in plaster directly from the death mask, and the back of the head was added. In the judgment of contemporaries it gives the truest impression of the founder's features. It lets us see how Ignatius actually looked: the man with a will of steel and a paternal goodness matured through suffering and then transfigured.

[100]

209 ▷

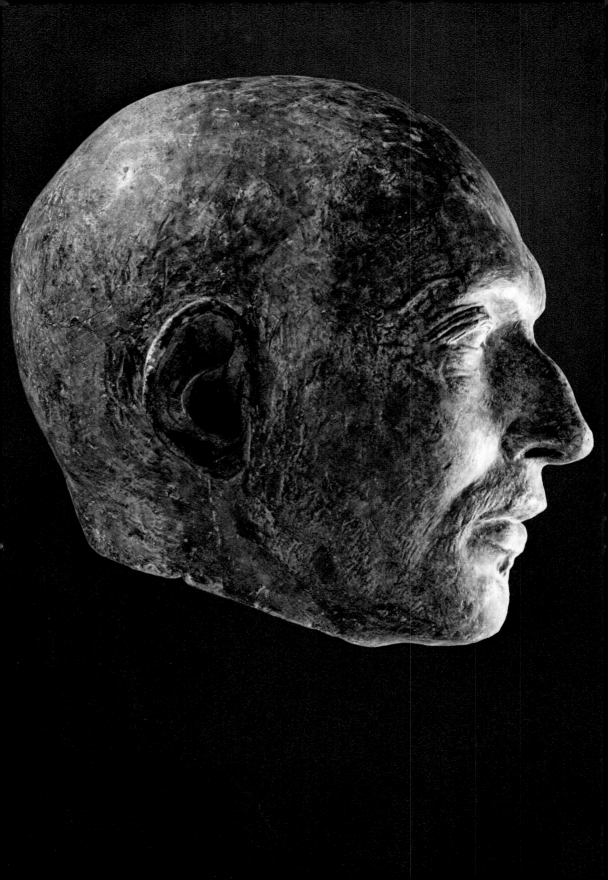

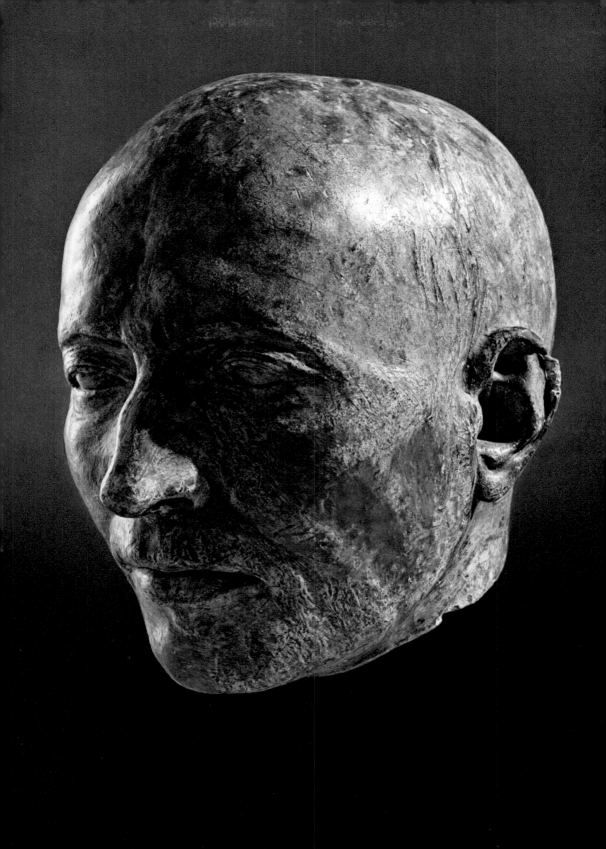

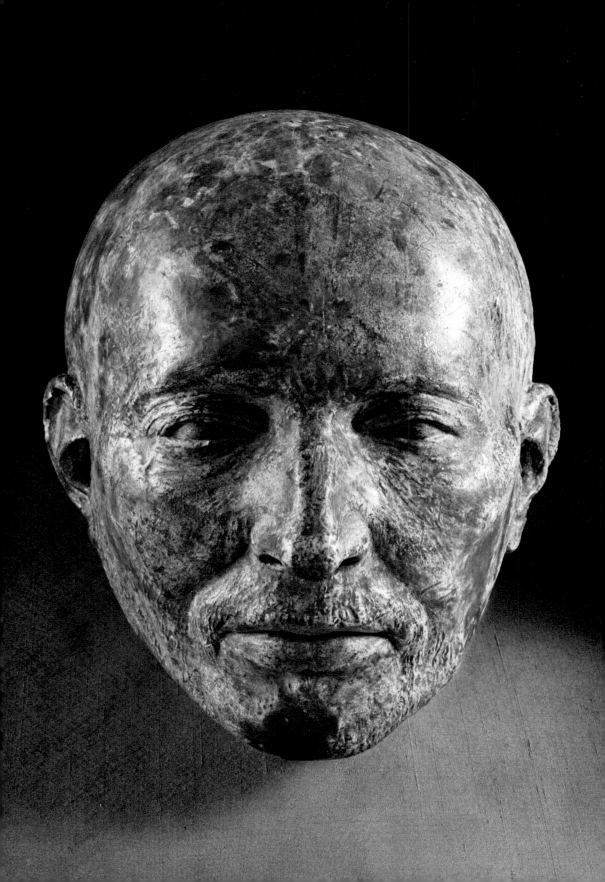

ALL FOR THE GREATER GLORY OF GOD

"The Christian world has lost one of its most distinguished leaders"; so wrote a Cardinal. That was the judgment of the whole world. Paul IV, otherwise no great friend of Loyola—on the occasion of his election in the previous year Ignatius had remarked, "All the bones in my body were trembling"—was deeply moved. Princes, noblemen, bishops, the Carthusians in Cologne and the pious Roman folk were all of the one conviction: a saint is dead. A year previously the city council of Barcelona had compared him with the great founders of Religious Orders and had written to him: "The day will come, we hope, when your memory will be held holy throughout the world." His brethren in far-off lands noted in their diaries the very same impression which Polanco had at Rome. "Our mourning is without sadness, our tears are rich with comfort, and though we grieve his loss we feel ourselves filled with spiritual joy." That is what happens when saints die.

In 1595 commenced the examination into his virtues in all the places in which Ignatius had lived. People streamed to pray piously at his new grave, prepared in 1587 in the church of the Gesù. It was there that Baronius in 1600 delivered his famous funeral oration. "We behold the leafy branches, the fruit and stem that is the Society of Jesus. But the root lies buried in the earth. And who is that root save Father Ignatius, who lies buried here in this spot beneath the earth?" On July 27th 1609 Ignatius was beatified. With joyful pride his homeland asked that "this sprig and son of the province of Guipúzcoa" should become its patron saint. On March 12th 1622 Ignatius was raised as a saint to the honours of the altar, together with the greatest of his sons, Francis Xavier. That was a glorious day for his Society.

The seventeenth century with its splendour of speech and art endeavoured to express in rich and vivid manner the greatness of this saint. The elaborate magnificence with which his tomb has been decorated since 1695, the splendid Basilica which since 1689 has stood by the side of the manor house at Loyola, the gleaming radiance of the ceiling frescoes of Pozzo in St Ignatius at Rome, this is all and only to express what the Society voices daily in a prayer to Ignatius: "O God, Thou alone art glorified through the glory of Thy saints." That is the legacy of this great saint who before God was small, and it is written on every page of the rules of his Society: "Everything to the greater glory of God."

ALL FOR THE GREATER GLORY OF GOD

Notes on the ten plates that follow:

217–218 SPLENDOUR ABOVE THE TOMB

The altar over the tomb in the Gesù at Rome was erected between 1695 and 1700. With its columns of lapis lazuli and gilded bronze it is one of the masterpieces of Baroque art. The silver statue was made in 1697 by Pierre le Gros. In 1798 it was partly destroyed, and the head and arms were restored in 1804 by Antonio Canova. The funeral urn of gilded bronze was designed by Alessandro Algardi in 1637.

219 TRIUMPH OF THE NAME OF JESUS

The ceiling fresco of the church of the Gesù, painted in 1672 by Gianbattista Gaulli, called Baciccio. Heaven, the earth and the underworld bow the knee, in the words of the Apostle Paul, before the Name of Jesus.

220–221 GO, AND SET THE WORLD ON FIRE

This saying of the saint inspired the Jesuit lay-brother, Andrea Pozzo, to create his famous ceiling fresco in the church of St Ignatius in Rome during the years 1686–1692. The light of the Eternal Father passes through the heart of His Son, carrying the Cross, to Ignatius, who radiates it to the four quarters of the world.

222, 223–224 HIS HOMELAND IS BLEST

In 1689 a start was made in accordance with the designs of the Roman architect Fontana, with the building of the magnificent church at Loyola and of the college which incorporates the saint's castle. Ignatius has indeed conferred an immortality upon his family name.

225–226 TO GOD ALONE THE HONOUR

Silver statue in the Basilica at Loyola. It was presented in 1741 by the "Royal Association of the Guipúzcoans in Caracas", in thanksgiving for the safe voyage of a ship, and was modelled in Rome by the Spanish artist, Francisco de Vergara the younger. The saint's finger points to the motto which alone explains the splendour of his life: To the Greater Glory of God.